Thrown into the Deep End...

A Journey of Faith

Charlene Ramirez

PublishAmerica
Baltimore

First printing

PublishAmerica has allowed this work to remain exactly as the author intended, verbatim, without editorial input.

Hardcover 978-1-4560-0197-1
Softcover 978-1-4560-0196-4
PUBLISHED BY PUBLISHAMERICA, LLLP
www.publishamerica.com
Baltimore

Printed in the United States of America

I wish to dedicate this book to my husband and friend, Sergio Ramirez. Thanks dear, for being part of of my life and part of this story. Your friendship and love has been a reflection of God's love, helping me to become the woman of God that I have become. Your support and encouragement has always meant so much. You are an amazing man of God, and I am blessed to be your wife.

In memorial:

During the writing of this book, I received the sad news that my dear friend, and first Pastor, Ronald Breaux, passed away. He taught me so much about spiritual things, and guided me through some of the hardest times of my life. The knowledge I have of the deeper spiritual things, I learned from this dear brother. His encouragement, his belief in my calling, gave me the strength to overcome my fears and insecurities and believe that God could use even me. I will deeply miss him.

PREFACE

As I look back, I am so thankful for the wonderful life the Lord has given me. I didn't always feel that way, in fact, for a great deal of my early years, I hated who I was. God really had a lot of work to do in me. My story is a testament to the faithfulness of God to take whatever we give Him and work with it. God is able to make something beautiful out of a train wreck. This book is written to give Him glory and thanks for all He has done in me and through me.

In telling my life story, I decided to dwell on the things that would be an encouragement to others and what would bring Glory to God. I focused on the good things God has done, rather than on the bad things I have done. I have read testimonies where the author goes into detail about the darkest sins in their lives. In a few cases it sounded as if they were bragging about how bad they were. The Word of God tells us "all have sinned and come short of the glory of God". We all have done things we regret. We all are ashamed of the many times we have failed God, so what is the purpose in discussing our shame and failure? One way or another, we have all been there and done things we are not proud of. Our sin is not the issue and should not be the focus of our life or our testimony, in my opinion, not if we have truly repented of it. God says He removes our sins from us, as far as the east is from the west. If He chooses to forgive and not remember it, I don't think He wants us to dwell on it either. Some people spend so much of their life in regret over the past, never forgiving themselves or others, that they continue to live in the past, never getting over the very thing that destroyed them. It's important to learn from our mistakes but not dwell on them. I remember once God gave a word in a service to someone. The word the Lord spoke through me to this individual was: "It is not important how many times you have failed, it is only important that you get up and try again." God wants us to be over-comers. He knows we are imperfect and we will fall over and over again. He made provision for our weakness, "I can do all things through Christ who strengthens me". Our failure should not destroy us, but remind us of our need to fully rely on Jesus to get things right.

This book is a testament to the greatness and goodness of God, His patience and love. One of the biggest revelations in my life was: even though I was an impossible mess for me to straighten out, I was not an impossible mess for God! The stories I share in this book are the ones I believe will minister to others who feel as lost and as hopeless as I once did. God transformed me from a person who hated herself to a person who loves her life and feels a source of pride and accomplishment in who she has become. God has taken me on an incredible journey. Everything that is good in my life is due to Him. The change in my attitude and my person are a result of the work His Spirit has done in my life through the Word of God and prayer. I know who I was and what I was capable of, and what I was incapable of, without Him. If anything, my story is a story on how God can take something that is useless to others and transform it into a blessing for many. Like the little boy's lunch, just a few small fish and some bread, in the hands of Jesus can become a feast that feeds thousands, so a life that has little to offer can become a life of purpose and blessing in the hands of the Lord. I live as a testament to this truth.

CHAPTER ONE
"The Early Years"

On a hot summer day in Tuscaloosa, Alabama, on June 24, 1952, my life began. My mother, Ellen Tomkins Davis, was working in the kitchen when she felt a slight twinge. Having given birth to my sister, Ellen Gail three years earlier, she didn't take the little pain too seriously at first. After all, I wasn't due for another five weeks. As the "twinges" continued and got closer together, she decided to make a call to my father, Charles Wallace Davis, or "Bud", as he was called. By the time he reached home from work, my mother knew it was time. On the way there, she was beginning to wonder if they would make it on time. As she told me the story, it seems I was in a hurry to arrive. My father was rather nervous, so instead of pulling up to the emergency room entrance, he parked in the parking lot! My mother said she was holding her stomach, half bent over in pain, as he assisted her through the parking lot towards the door. She said every time she looked up it seemed as if it was farther away. When they entered the emergency room, she was immediately whisked away while my father filled out the papers. It was around 2:15pm when they arrived. She said she kept telling the nurses the baby was coming now, as they went up in the elevator to the maternity ward. When the nurse checked, she realized my mother was correct, so as the elevator doors opened, they entered the first room, which happened to be a storage room, and that's where I was born, at 2:25pm! My father hadn't even finished filling out the paperwork when they came to tell him he had a daughter.

I weighed a little less than five pounds, so I had to stay in the hospital for a couple of weeks, but otherwise I was a healthy baby girl, somewhat thin, but healthy nonetheless for a preemie. They named me Charlene W. Davis. I was named after my father. My sister had been named after my mother. The problem was they couldn't think of a name they liked that began with a "W", so I ended up with just an initial instead of a middle name, something I never appreciated. It was awkward when the kids would ask my middle name and I had to explain I just had a letter. My mother said because I was premature she had to feed me almost every hour at first; but by the time I was six months old, I was such a butterball I couldn't sit up without pillows around me to prop me up!

When I was around two years old, I developed a very bad cough and had difficulty breathing. At the time, my mother said the doctor thought it was asthma. We found out years later through some series of tests that I actually had a lung disease from the Tuberculosis family, called Histoplasmosis. Somehow I healed from it without being properly treated for it, which was a miracle in itself, however, it did leave scar tissue behind which would cause me problems later on in life.

My parents were wonderful people, totally devoted to each other and to us girls. We were a very happy family. My father had gone through some rough times in his childhood, but he was a good man, and a good father. He was a quiet man, but he loved to play with us and helped with our care. My mother was a stay at home mom. I was blessed with a loving family, even my older sister doted over me when I was little. My mother said I was a very peaceful child. I would play for hours at her feet. She said I had a tremendous imagination and could entertain myself for hours. I always seemed content, as long as my mother was in view.

My mother had been a church goer when she was a child, but my father was not a church going man. My mother was always there for us and especially for my dad. When he was home, she was there to be with him. Since he didn't like to go to church, we didn't go very often either. On occasion we would go to a neighborhood church, but in my early years our family was not regular church attenders. My problems did not stem from coming from a broken home, or physical or emotional abuse. I had a wonderful family. The weakness in my character came from me. I had an emotional weakness, a handicap in my ability to deal with my emotions. I can only compare it to the experience I have seen in planting a garden. The soil is healthy and prepared. You plant seeds that look the same, yet one plant thrives, and the other is frail. It never seems to develop the strength in it's stem. It needs to have a stick to support it, if not, it will bend, cutting off the circulation of the nutrients it needs to grow. With a lot of care it can still produce, but it needs help and attention to do so. That was me. I realize now, I needed Christ in my life from the beginning. I needed that support. I am glad God designed me with this weakness now, as I realize it was what compelled me to seek Him. Being grafted in to Christ, has made Him my strength and support. In Christ I have become what I never could have become on my own. All the things which went wrong in my life led me to realize the great need I had of Him, so I am indeed thankful.

When I was six years old my father received a job offer to become a plant manager, but it would involve moving to another country. My father worked for B. F. Goodrich. They offered him a position in Lima, Peru. The economy there would offer them a great opportunity to save money and get ahead, so he accepted the job. I still remember the trip to Peru. It was in the summer of 1958; well, it was summer here, but it was the winter season there. We flew on a propeller plane, as it was before the time of jets. We flew all night, making stops in Panama and Ecuador to refuel. We arrived, when the sun was coming up, to a world that was totally different from anything I had ever experienced.

People looked different and spoke in a language I couldn't understand. Even though it was winter there, it was not very cold. Lima's climate is very similar to Southern California's. There were people who were strangely dressed selling all kinds of things everywhere you looked. They were Inca Indians my mother told me. I was totally amazed by these people. They smiled at me and though I couldn't understand their words, I understood their expressions. They showed me a great deal of love and attention. I was a blond haired little girl with green eyes, which was a rare thing for them to see. At any rate, my first impression of the Hispanic people was a very positive one.

We went to stay at a wonderful place that looked like a palace to me. Actually, it was the Country Club of Lima. It was a stately looking place with wonderful gardens and large verandas. It had so many places to explore. Although the pool area was closed for the season, the gardens and grounds were kept up. There were peacocks roaming the gardens, along with other wildlife. It was a magical playground. My sister and I loved it there. We stayed for several weeks until my parents found a house for us. It was nothing like the small home we had in Alabama. This house had five bedrooms, three bathrooms, servant quarters, and a guest room out back. We suddenly had the life of the affluent, with a maid, chauffeur, and a gardener. Even though our lifestyle had changed, mother made sure we still had to keep our rooms clean and help out, so we wouldn't get spoiled for when we moved back to the States.

I began school in Lima, at Franklin Delano Roosevelt School. It was a private, all English speaking school for grades K-12. So, even though we were in a foreign country, we stayed within an American community. I learned some Spanish, as they taught a class twice a week, but it was basics for first graders, like colors, days, simple phrases. I loved it in Peru, as did my sister, but my mother said she always wanted to go home. There was so much to do and see for a child. We lived in an area where many of the affluent foreign businessmen and their families lived. There were many English speaking children to play with, so it was a fun adventure for us, rather than a traumatic experience.

The school was a close knit society. Since it covered all age groups, whole families went there. My sister, who was always very mature for her age, was just entering her teen years She was more athletic and socially outgoing than I was. She played on the volley ball team, and was always busy in some activity. I spent a lot of time playing by myself or with a few friends I had in the neighborhood. It amazes me, as I look back, how times have changed. Here we were, living in a foreign country, and I would go off for hours roaming the neighborhood, visiting a nearby park, or walking over to a friend's house, without parental supervision. Not that my parents were uninvolved or neglectful, it was just a different time. Back then, you could let your children play outside without having to watch them, or let them go unescorted to different places. It gave you a sense of freedom and adventure that I believe is sadly missing in today's society. Because of the horrible crimes we read about, we shelter our children from so many wonderful experiences in order to protect them. At any rate, living in Peru was like living in a paradise for me. I have wonderful memories of great adventures. Our family went to see Inca ruins; we took trips into the Andes; we went to bull fights, which I didn't enjoy much, as I always wanted the bull to win. We ate at the finest restaurants and had parties and events to attend. In all, it was a very exciting time.

After we had been there a couple of years, my father became ill. It started as a pain in the back of his leg. It was later determined he had a blood clot, and he underwent surgery to remove it. Unfortunately, the medical facilities there were not up to par. What was to be a relatively safe procedure, turned for the worse when unclean conditions caused gangrene to set in. My father became very ill. His foot turned black. At that point, the company sent him back to the States to a specialist. He was so ill that he had to fly on a stretcher with a private nurse accompanying him. We all flew back. I don't think I realized how serious it was. When we arrived, my grandparents were at the airport to meet us. My mother went to the hospital with my father, and we went to stay on my grandparents farm in Paoli, Pennsylvania. This was the first time I had ever been separated from them. I was very sensitive and attached to my mother in particular, so it was a very hard time for me.

I loved their old farmhouse. It was built in 1775. It was about the greatest place on earth. I loved going out to take care of the animals with my grandpa. My grandmother, however, was not very affectionate. My sister was into watching American Bandstand and loved to watch television in English, (something that we didn't get too much of in Peru). I followed my grandpa around most of the day, or played with the dog or the kittens. Still, I was very lonely, not having any children my age around and worse yet, not having my parents around. A couple of month's past by, which seemed like an eternity to me. One day my sister ran past me crying and wouldn't talk to me. I kept asking my grandmother what was wrong, but she wouldn't tell me. She just said my sister didn't feel good. What had really happened was they had given her the news about my father. They thought I was too young to understand, so they didn't tell me. My father had almost passed away, and in order to save his life, they amputated his leg.

In those days, I spent a lot of time off on the farm wandering around. One day, when I was particularly sad about not seeing my parents, I climbed a large hill in a wooded area. As I reached the top, I found a large rock to sit and rest on. I just sat there looking up at the sky. I always believed in God. I don't know if it came from the few times I went to church, or the Bible story books I had read, or my mother teaching me to say "now I lay me down to sleep" each night. I just believed He was there. As I sat on this rock, I sensed His presence. I didn't see anyone, but I felt there was someone there with me. I heard a voice as if it was speaking into my soul, letting me know I was not alone, I was loved, and there was a special purpose in my life. The voice assured me that He would always be with me, and I didn't need to be afraid. That's about all I remember, but somehow I knew it was Jesus. I remember telling Him I loved Him, but an event that would soon happen would rob me of this wonderful early memory for many years.

Several weeks later, we took a trip on Easter to see my parents for the first time in 3 months. It was wonderful to see them. I was so excited. At lunchtime my mother took us down to the hospital cafeteria for lunch. On the way to the elevator, she remembered she had forgotten her purse and needed to go back to the room to get it. I ran ahead, shouting I would get it for her. I didn't listen to her shouting for me to stop as I raced back down the hall to daddy's room. I entered the room to see my father, who previously had been in bed under the covers, sitting up in a chair, but he only had one leg. The scarred stub was right in front of me. I went into shock. I thought I said "why are you sitting on your leg?", but my mother said I actually said, "why did you let them cut your leg off". Funny how the mind shuts down when it doesn't understand. All I know is that when I ran out of the room with my mother's purse, it took a few minutes for it to dawn on me what I had just seen. I began to cry and became hysterical. I wanted to go back to tell my daddy it was okay, I loved him anyway, and how sorry I was, but my mother thought it was better that she spend some time alone with me. I didn't go back to tell him. Somehow in my mind I thought from that point on that somehow I had hurt him. I wouldn't sit on his lap or go near him much after that. I was afraid I would hurt him. It was a trauma that would set in motion many problems in my life. From that point on I had very little memory of anything that had happened prior. For years I could not remember my father playing with me when I was a child, or how I felt about anything. It was as if I went into some dark cave that would take me years to come out of. I forgot many things, including the encounter with Jesus on the hill that day, but He never forgot me.

When my father was finally better, we returned to Peru, but we weren't there for very long until the trauma I had experienced began to show its effects. Shortly after we returned, I had an incident where I stiffened up and passed out. No one took it too seriously. I had problems at school the last year I was there. It was fourth grade, and my teacher was very insensitive and cruel to me. I suddenly didn't like school anymore. When we returned to the United States, I began having problems with horrible stomach cramps from time to time. They thought I had Colitis. All these different health issues began to appear. I had always had a weakness in my respiratory system. I caught colds very easily, and they quickly turned into bronchitis. On top of that, I began to mature very early, at ten years of age, and I had horrible cramps almost every month. When someone has a lot of emotional issues, a lot of stress, adding hormonal changes at such an early age on top of it all, was the worst thing that could have happened. I am mentioning these issues as part of the testimony of the things God has done for me and the many things He has healed me from.

Life in Akron, Ohio, where we settled upon returning from Peru, was very different. I was seen as an oddity by most of the children in my class. They made up silly little rhymes about me. Children can be so cruel at times. They found it very odd that I came from a foreign country. I didn't feel like I fit in very well. I was ten when we returned. A year later, President Kennedy was shot. I was a dreamer, always looking for the beauty in everything, and the rejection I felt from my schoolmates as well as coming face to face with the evil that exists in this world, was more than I knew how to handle. My health issues continued. My mother would often tell me that I needed to not be so sensitive, I needed to "toughen up" she said. But I always felt if I had to become cruel like others, I would rather not live. I looked at the world with rose colored glasses. I began writing poetry to put into words my confusion with life.

Then the Beatles became a big hit, and I, like most young ladies, was fascinated with them. I started making some friends who were fans as well. Things were a little better for me socially at least. At the same time we were studying world cultures in school, and I started looking into different religions and beliefs. For awhile, I started to believe in reincarnation, but eventually decided it was ridiculous. I tried to read the Bible, but I couldn't understand it. I remember watching a movie about a nun, and thought perhaps I should become a nun some day. I also got a hold of some medical books and read them, thinking I might be a doctor. I had this overwhelming desire to do something to help humanity, but I didn't have any idea what it was. I was fascinated with crosses, and treasured the cross with a real diamond chip in it which my parents bought me for Christmas. The things of God always called my attention. I remember when I was younger in Peru, anytime my friends and I found a dead animal or bug, we would bury it and have a funeral service for it, and I was always the preacher who said the final words and the prayer. I guess I always had this call to do something for others in my life. My mother use to tell me I should join the peace corps when I grew up.

My thoughts would go too deep at times. I over-analyzed everything. I found out it made me different, unpopular, so I began to keep it to myself. I hid my feelings, covering it up with doing whatever would keep me busy or distract me from thinking or feeling. I had a tremendous imagination, which allowed me to escape all the negative emotions I found so difficult to deal with. I learned how to make friends and be accepted; I had to adapt. I became a people-pleaser, but covering up who you really are has consequences.

My sister was in High School at the time. She and I weren't very close, partly because she was almost 4 years older, but also because we were so different in nature. She had lots of friends, mostly older than her. She was always so mature. I was a pretty young girl, but acted rather odd compared to most. Still, for a time, my sister and I started to hang out some. I was a pre-teen, suddenly interested in music and dancing, and she started to take me along with her. It made me feel grown-up. It was cool to hang out with her, but that ended when some of the older boys started to pay too much attention to me.

She was always very protective of me. I remember a time when a neighborhood boy, who was her age, whistled at me and made some comments. The next day, at school, she cornered him by his locker and let him know if he ever whistled or talked to her little sister like that again, he would have to answer to her. The boy never looked at me after that. I was proud to have her look out for me. She decided for my own good, to stop taking me along when the older boys started noticing me, (I had developed early and was very naive). Still, it made me sad not being included anymore. I had wanted to be close to my sister for a long time, and for awhile, I thought things had changed. I felt like I must have messed things up again. Whenever things went wrong, I always blamed myself. I didn't realize she was actually just looking out for me.

The Davis family:
Charles, "Bud" Davis, Ellen Davis, Gail (right), Charlene (left) age 5

CHAPTER TWO
"The Terrible Teens"

If I thought childhood was difficult, I had no idea what trauma the teen years would bring, and the added hormone surges didn't make it any easier. Entering Junior High at first didn't seem so bad. It was a larger school, so I could kind of get lost in the crowd. I buried myself in music and dancing. It was a language that enabled me to interact and communicate with other kids, without having to reveal too much of the inner me. I discovered it was a great way to turn off the serious side, and just relax and have fun. It was a relief to be able to just have fun and not think about things; I have some fond memories of those times. I had finally managed to escape my more serious side and enjoy life, but then the complication of relationships with boys began.

When I turned fourteen God visited me again. One night I was in bed and saw this light in the corner of my room which began to get larger and larger. A form dressed in a white robe appeared, but the face was too bright to see. I could see the arms outstretched towards me, and I noticed scars in the hands. I was so frightened that I hid under the covers. I kept saying, "Please don't hurt me; please go away." I didn't know what it was, perhaps a ghost. I realize now it was the Lord. After awhile, I got up the courage to peek out from the covers and it was gone. I ran downstairs to my mother to tell her. I thought she would think I was dreaming, or just making it up, but she looked at me seriously and told me she believed I had seen something by the expression on my face. I didn't know what she meant by that, but I was glad she believed me. If I had known to be still and just talk to God, or remembered how he spoke to me years earlier on the mountain, perhaps things would have been different. I look back now and realize before each critical moment in my life, he was reaching out to me. Not long after, I passed out while in school several times. My mother took me to a doctor who put me in the hospital to run some tests. They found out I had a form of epilepsy called psycho-motor epilepsy. They also discovered spots on my lungs from scar tissue from the lung disease I had as a child. It amazed the doctors that I had recovered from it without being treated.

I had liked boys for quite awhile and had a few little boyfriends, but nothing serious. Then I met a boy that I fell head over heals for. It was my first love. We were very serious about each other. Of course, I thought we would run off and get married when we turned sixteen, but after eight months, he broke up with me. I was devastated. I didn't know how to deal with the hurt. All of the depression and hurt I had managed to cover up came back with a vengeance. Unfortunately, my self-destructive behavior led me to criticize and blame myself. I never had the capability of lashing out and hurting others, but I was cruel and relentless on myself. One evening, in a moment of desperation, I cut my wrists. Once again, I had messed up something beautiful. I was a failure at love, just like I felt I had been at everything else. Fortunately, God was watching over me. I didn't cut deep enough, and I clotted quickly. I had done this before going to bed, thinking I would slowly bleed to death and never wake up, but I woke up the next day, and honestly, I was relieved. I started thinking if I had died it would have really hurt my family, and I didn't want them to suffer because of me.

I spent a year in such a depression over the breakup. Eventually, I slowly started to date again, but I never really got over it. The next boyfriends I had were all similar, as if I was trying to replace him, but unfortunately, they were as unfaithful as he had been. I think I was just trying to get that wonderful feeling of being in love back again. I wish I would have opened up with my parents about what was going on inside, or gotten help, but the fear of being rejected kept me from letting anyone see the real me inside. Anyone I had let get in a little hurt me. I believed I was so messed up, so ugly on the inside, that it was better to keep it to myself. (I have found out in living life, there are so many young people going through these problems. The worst thing is when you're young, you think there's something wrong with just you, and the rest of the world is fine, so you never reach out to try to get help. Some how, you think no one else will understand.)

My biggest problem was dealing with rejection. I had strong convictions, and had been raised with a good sense of morals, but this was the sixties. The whole world was turning upside down. The Vietnam War was wreaking havoc on the youth of our nation. It was a time of protest, of free love, of the birth of the rock age and drug culture. While I continued to try to be the young lady my parents had raised me to be, the pressure from my friends and the culture was overwhelming. I wanted to be accepted, to fit it, to belong. I couldn't stand any kind of rejection, not from my parents, and not from my friends, so I began living two lives. I was what my parents wanted, and I was what my friends wanted. I tried to please everyone, and lost myself in the process. I began to hate myself for being such a phony, such a pushover. I was convinced that if my parents knew, they wouldn't love me anymore (which was not true), and if I stopped going out with my friends they would make fun of me, and they wouldn't love me anymore either. I lost all respect for myself.

As I look back now, I don't know why I felt the way I did. My father was a quiet man, who came home, talked to my mother, and then sat down to read the paper. If you talked to him, it was usually through the paper, and even though he would say, "uh-huh", you got the feeling he wasn't really listening or interested. I really didn't speak to him too much, (which I found out later really bothered him). I was a momma's girl. My mother was always there to listen. I remember coming home and sitting on the kitchen counter talking to her while she was cooking. I would tell her all about my friends and their problems, or about school. She really listened. She knew all my friends names, and would keep up with all the new developments. I found it so easy to tell her about all of them, but so hard to tell her what was going on inside of me. While my father was somewhat critical at times, she never was. She was always supportive. I really don't know why I felt I couldn't confide the deepest things in my heart to her. I think I needed her love and approval so much that I felt if I disappointed her I would lose it. I know now the enemy was working to destroy me, and deceived me into not reaching out to the people who really loved me and could help me.

My health declined, as I was smoking and it made my lung problems worse. I had pneumonia twice and eight lung infections in a two year period. I tried to quit smoking, but my nerves were so damaged that I shook all the time and it seemed to be the only thing that calmed me down. Some strange "blackouts" I had, as a result of the epilepsy, convinced me I was loosing my mind. I had nightmares about being locked in an mental hospital. I began to believe it would be better to be dead than to end up in a place like that. I thought I was having a breakdown, so I went as an outpatient to a psychiatric hospital. They diagnosed me with several conditions, and suggested I needed to make a break and start over new. So I went home and told my parents I was going crazy and I needed to get away. My girlfriend and I wanted to go to Florida. My father was overwhelmed that I had gone to see a Psychiatrist. He couldn't understand why I hadn't told them about the problems I was having, but how could I? If I told them my deepest secrets, I thought they would be so disappointed in me. I just couldn't talk to them. I felt like I would be letting them down. My mother seemed to understand why I sought out a professional and tried to convince him. I felt so awful for disappointing him, I just wanted to run away. They just wanted to see me happy and if the doctor thought I should get away, they agreed to let me go. My friend and I left for Florida, but my problems there were no different than my problems in Ohio. You can't run away from who you are. After a few short weeks, I returned home. My parents had redecorated my room, to welcome me home. At least I felt good that they wanted me back, but I still felt as if I was a failure and didn't deserve their love.

I was seventeen and a mess, so I decided again to try to end it all. I hated school; I hated life. Everyone I had ever known had hurt me in one way or the other, and it just didn't seem worth living if life was just one painful experience after another. It was December of 1969. I remember looking out of my bedroom window. I cried out to God in prayer. I remember the prayer: "Jesus, I hear you are the Son of God, and I believe it, because I want to believe someone like you really exists. If you are the Son of God, then you're perfect, and that means you wouldn't hurt me like everyone else has. If you could please just love me, I will give you my life and do whatever you want me to do, but if you don't want to love me, please just let me die in peace tonight." The prayer was my last ditch effort for help.

The sad thing is I went to school with two pastor's daughters. No one ever told me the plan of salvation or told me Jesus loved me. I had never heard the term "born again". I had no idea there was a way for my sins to be forgiven. I didn't know Jesus loved me, I just hoped He would. I didn't hear His voice that night, I didn't see any sign, but I no longer felt like killing myself. Two weeks later while I was working after school, a person came into where I worked and told me about God's love and the plan of salvation. When he told me all I had to do was ask Jesus to forgive me and give Him my life, I remember telling him I had already done that. He was amazed that I did it without even knowing why. I was overwhelmed hearing the words that Jesus loved me ALL THE TIME! That was all I ever wanted, someone who really knew me and still loved me. Then he told me about my name being written in the book of life and because of this I would be with Jesus in Heaven forever! What a surprise! I was just looking for someone to love me for the here and now, and I found out it would be for all eternity! And thus began the great love affair of my life with Jesus.

Now, I am not saying that I was instantly changed, or that I instantly stopped some of my bad habits. I didn't know anything about the Word of God, or what God expected from me. I visited a church which was a fundamental evangelical church. I listened to every word. I enrolled in a Bible class. I wanted to learn. Little by little, I began to learn what was good and what was not. I became very passionate about my faith, to the exclusion of everything else. Now, I'm not saying that's a bad thing, but sometimes we lack wisdom and can become downright overbearing. I had found a purpose, a mission in life. The desire I had for all those years to do something good for others now had a focus. I knew I was suppose to share the good news of God's love with others. Unfortunately, not everyone shares your enthusiasm. I tried to reach my family, especially my father and sister. My mother had always had faith in Christ, from an early age. She was happy to see me find purpose in my new found faith, and she was very supportive. I am sure my obsessive behavior was tolerated by her because it was better than being involved with the drug culture and political protests of the time. She was glad to see me involved and happy with something which was positive. My father had never been a man of faith. When he was a young man, he worked with an evangelical Christian who liked to preach fire and brimstone to him. He said this man was very pushy, and it really turned him off. My sister was not the least bit interested at the time in anything "religious". So, I got on their nerves pretty quick. I can remember comments like, "Can't you talk about something else for a change?", and "There she goes again!" I was so happy, so in love with Jesus, I wanted everyone to know Him. What I didn't realize is "sharing" and "shoving" are two different things. I began to notice they would leave the room when I started talking about Jesus.

I still had the problem of wanting people to like me, and I still kept looking for the "one", my prince charming. I had Jesus in my life, but I also wanted to find someone, with the hopes of one day getting married and starting a family. I began dating a young man who claimed he was a Christian. He had been at Bible college and he encouraged me to go. The longer we dated, the more controlling he became. I decided to go off to a Bible College in North Carolina. It was an entirely different world there. These were people who were missionary kids, pastor's kids, people brought up in the gospel. It was a Southern Baptist Bible College, and their doctrine was very different to me. It seemed as if everything was wrong to do. I had a hard time fitting in there; after all, I was the only "Yankee", as they called me. Still, the classes were good, and I learned a lot. I missed home, especially my mom. There was an issue which developed at the time, in order for the school to receive state funding they would have to open admission to everyone. It blew me away to see the reaction of some of these kids to the thought of accepting other races at school. These were students studying to be pastors and missionaries, and they didn't want to go to school with other races. The hypocrisy really upset me and I let them know. I decided it was not the place for me. I've learned through the years that not everyone who says I'm a Christian always truly follows Christ.

I went back home really confused. I wanted to serve God, but I couldn't find the place that was right for me. My relationship with this young man became more abusive and eventually ended tragically. In the midst of all this, I was like a ship lost in a big ocean. I didn't know which way to go or what I was suppose to do. At nineteen I was in love with Jesus, but just as confused and hurt with people as I had ever been. I still had not come to terms with who I was. I loved the Lord, but I didn't love me. It would take many years for God to undo the tangled mess I had going on inside, but the Bible says, "Who the son sets free, is free indeed." The process of changing our way of thinking is not an overnight task, but I am so thankful the good work He began in me, He was faithful to complete.

Charlene after graduation with her favorite car

CHAPTER THREE
"Becoming a Wife and Mother"

I was nineteen years old, but I thought I was all grown up. In a way, I was. I had gone through a lot of things throughout my teen years. Adversity has a way of maturing you, but I don't think I was at all ready to be a wife or mother. Nevertheless, it seems it was all I wanted out of life. I think I felt I was a failure at everything else, and that was all that remained for me. I always loved the thought of having children. I was still searching for unconditional love, and perhaps I thought I would achieve it as a wife and mother.

There was a young man, who I met while in the tragic relationship I had been in. He had been a mutual friend, who started coming around to see me. Eventually he told me he had been in love with me while I was dating the other guy and he didn't like how the other guy treated me, but he never had the courage to say anything. At the time, I wasn't going to church like I had been before. I was a little let down from the "Bible College" experience. Not that I was disappointed with Jesus, just with those who said they were Christians. It was a confusing time for me. But being resentful and judgmental of others didn't put me in a right standing with God. There I was, lost, lonely, looking for love, so I married the first man who said he loved me and wanted to marry me. I was grateful someone wanted me. I was in love with the idea of being in love, "the happily ever after" story all little girls dream of. I kept thinking if I would just find the right guy, it would make everything alright. Why is it we think someone else can fix us? I knew there was something in me that needed to change, to be healed, but instead of getting help to fix me, I thought I could fix it by getting married and having kids. I knew shortly thereafter that I had made a mistake. I knew I should have waited on the Lord to show me what His will was, but I didn't. Now I had to deal with the fact that I was married and so I decided the only right thing to do was to do my best to make it work.

I really tried to be a good wife in the beginning, but not long after we were married, he changed. He became quiet and withdrawn. I was certain I had failed once again. It didn't seem I could do anything right. I wasn't right with the Lord when I met him, if I had been, perhaps I would have made different choices. I'm not saying it was all his fault. It's unrealistic to think a person can make you whole, or make you feel worth something. He had been married before, and had gone through some very traumatic experiences himself. Perhaps he thought marrying me would fix his problems. I think he was on the rebound as well, and somehow he thought marrying me would make things alright, until he woke up and realized I wasn't his ex-wife and he couldn't change me into being her. At the time, I was sure I was to blame and beat myself up over it. That was such a part of my nature for so many years, always blaming myself for everything. I punished myself for so long, I didn't know any other way to be, so I was certain there must be something I was doing wrong. I still had the concept, "if I am good enough, he will love me". I tried to win his affection back, thinking it might change our relationship, by doing the things he wanted to do. I started to go to the clubs with him and tried to live in his world. We had fun for awhile, but deep inside I felt more lost. It was as if I was on a path going in reverse. As I got farther away from the Lord, the worse things got inside me. We were two broken people hoping the other one would fix what was wrong in us. We had so much baggage that the relationship was doomed from the start. When I became pregnant with my first child, I finally felt I would have someone in my life who would love me no matter what. All that mattered to me, from that point on, was my baby. I decided it was time to return to the Lord. I stopped following my husband's lifestyle and I returned to church, which distanced us from each other even more.

After thirty hours of labor, my first son, Chad, was born. I finally felt I had done something right. For the first time I had someone who loved me no matter who I was. His little eyes looked up at me with so much love. I was mom. He didn't care about my past, who I was or wasn't. I poured all my love into that child. It was him and me against the world.

My commitment to the Lord began to grow as I spent hours a day in the Word and in prayer. I had heard somewhere that there was over seven thousand promises in the Word of God. I wanted to know them all! I started a journal in which I wrote down all the scriptures of promise I found in the Bible. Every time I would put my son to sleep I would open the Word of God. I would spend hours in study and in prayer. I found I would sometimes fall asleep when I tried to pray, so I started writing God "prayer letters". I found if I wrote my prayers down, I wouldn't fall asleep. I poured my heart out in those letters. I wish I would have kept them but somehow they were lost along the way, still, I am thankful the Lord led me to spend those hours in study and prayer.

It was in those times that I heard God's voice again. It sounded familiar. Suddenly the blinders that had robbed me for so many years of my memories began to fall away. I remembered the encounter I had with Him on the hilltop when I was only eight. I realized He had been there with me all along. It was a time of renewal and re-commitment for me. What was even greater was the insight becoming a parent gave me. I suddenly was able to comprehend the depth of love my parents had for me, and greater still, the depth of love God felt for me. The knowledge of all this began healing what was broken inside, but it was no instant fix; the trials and lessons were just beginning.

My son was only six months old when I began feeling weak. I went to a doctor, then to a specialist. They discovered that the scar tissue from the lung disease I had as a child had begun to grow. It was pressing against the main artery coming out of my heart. It was a very rare condition. They told me I could not get pregnant again or take birth control as the hormones would make the growth get bigger. They believed the hormone changes in my first pregnancy provoked the scar tissue to begin to grow. I was devastated thinking I couldn't have any more children, and their long term prognosis for my condition wasn't very comforting either. They told me the drugs available could help but might cause serious kidney damage, and I already had problems with kidney infections. Surgery was an option, but a very dangerous procedure, and they couldn't guarantee the scar tissue wouldn't grow back again. They decided my best option was to wait and intervene with surgery when it became absolutely necessary. I had a six month old baby and suddenly I worried I would not be able to care for him or be around to see him grow up. Needless to say, my faith was shaken, but the Word of God that I had been studying gave me comfort and assurance. Somehow I knew God would see me through this trial.

Since I felt that my son was the only thing I had ever done right, I latched onto him like a drowning man latches onto a life preserver. Unfortunately, I made him the center of my universe, the reason for my being, which was not the place God wanted me to be. I still dealt with a great deal of fear. I became very over-protective of my son, battling the "what ifs" on a daily basis.

One night I had this dream where some men in masks came and took my child and told me to deny Christ or they would kill him. It was a horrible nightmare. I woke up in a sweat. I convinced myself it was just a terrible nightmare the devil had given me. But I couldn't get the dream out of my mind. I had always prayed that God would never take the one person who really loved me out of my life, not my baby.

31

I begged him never to put me to that test, and here was this dream that wouldn't let go. It kept popping into my mind for days. Finally, I asked God to help it go away. To my surprise God asked me, "Which one would you choose?" I remember saying, "This can't be from you; you would never ask me to choose", but the question kept coming back to me over and over. I realized it was my "Abraham" moment. God tested Abraham by asking him to sacrifice Isaac. Isaac had become the apple of his eye, the thing he held most dear. God wanted Abraham to realize he had placed his son in first place in priority in his heart. I had done the same with my son. In that moment, the dream became real to me, as if it were really happening, and I knew God was asking me to choose who would be first in my life, Him or my child. I wrestled with the answer until I finally surrendered in tears. I came to the understanding that my child was a gift God's love had sent me, but the gift should never be more important than the one who gave it. I chose God, and prayed I would never have to face the test in reality.

Your walk with God is not always an instant success. We take so many detours. There are so many ups and downs, so many choices along the way. You may grow, spiritually speaking, in the knowledge of God, and still be a mess emotionally. It takes time and yielding for the Holy Spirit to rearrange your thought process. I was in love with God, but I still didn't love myself.

As I look back, the saddest thing is how little self worth I had. It took God years of work to get me to the point where I could see myself with the right eyes. Our identity is not in who's wife we are, or who's mother we are. It isn't in our accomplishments or talents. A career or success, the people in our life, none of these things are a measure of who we are in the eyes of God. He loves us as unique individuals regardless of how we "perform". Why are we so hard on ourselves? After all, we are not experts at being human. Each one of us is learning to "be" for the first time. Why do we expect we will be perfect at it? If I could go back and teach myself one truth I think it would be to "lighten up", and not be so self condemning. If someone who is reading this can identify with who I was, do yourself a favor and give yourself a break. You are God's child, and as a child, you're going to make plenty of mistakes. Everyone does, and God is okay with that. Learn to accept yourself for who you are and realize God loves you just the way you are. You will save yourself a lot of heartache and condemnation. The hardest person to forgive sometimes is yourself. God is perfect, without sin, and if He can forgive you, than you need to do it too. God is much more interested in the lesson you learn from your mistakes than the mistake itself. (This is just a little advice from someone who wishes she had heard it years ago.)

CHAPTER FOUR
"The Holy Spirit Visits My Life"

There was a home group from my church which met every week. I had become friends with the leaders. They taught the older youth, and I taught the middle school kids, so they were mentors to me. I began to attend their home group, and the presence of the Lord in that place was tremendous. This couple had such a peace. They were always so steady, so Christ-like. I was speaking to the sister on the phone one day and I asked her how come my life was so up and down, spiritually speaking. I was on fire one week, and depressed and down in the dumps the next. She asked me a strange question, "Have you received the Holy Spirit since you believed?" I wasn't sure how to answer. She began to talk to me about the book of Acts and of Pentecost. I thought asking Jesus into your life was all you had to do. I had been at a Southern Baptist Bible College which taught Pentecost was for that time, speaking in tongues was then, not now. As she explained it to me, she could tell it was not the doctrine I had been previously taught. She told me to go and read the book of Acts, especially chapter nineteen, and pray about it. I got off the phone a bit confused, but I couldn't deny she had something I didn't have.

I read chapter nineteen, and sure enough, there were some who believed in Christ, but Paul asked them if they had received the Holy Spirit SINCE they believed. It was not something that happened simultaneously. Upon being prayed for, these believers received the Holy Spirit with the evidence of speaking in tongues. There it was! This sister had told me that her walk with Jesus had been up and down until she received the Holy Spirit, and He had given her peace, power to witness, and an understanding of the Word of God, all the things I so desperately needed. I decided to pray right then and there. I knew the Word of God said, "What father among you, if your child asks for bread will give him a stone, and if we, being evil, know how to give good gifts to our children, how much more our Heavenly Father will give the Holy Spirit to them that ask." So I reasoned in my heart, if I asked Jesus for the Holy Spirit, He would answer my prayer. If it wasn't an experience from God, He wouldn't give it to me. I asked in faith. I sat there praising God for a few minutes. I heard a word in my mind, the word "Abba". At first it crossed my mind that I was making it up, but then I corrected myself by thinking, "you asked in faith, so believe". I opened my mouth and said the word I heard, several times, and then I started speaking in another language, perhaps a paragraph or two, but there it was. I wondered afterward if it was for real, or my imagination, but it had happened. I felt a peace about it all, but I had no idea what was the purpose, and I thought it was just a one time event. I had so little experience. I had been a Christian for seven years, but I had never heard any teaching about such things. I went to an Fundamental Evangelical church, a Baptist school, and now I was in a Presbyterian church. I had never heard about the gifts of the Spirit or about healing. Still, something happened immediately after that experience. The painful cramps I had endured every month for over ten years never returned after that day. I also was healed from the epilepsy and no longer had to take medication. God had given me evidence something had happened. I didn't know to pray for healing, so I think the Holy Spirit must have prayed for me, and I was healed. God was healing me in other ways too, I just didn't know it until later.

My marriage however, was still like being on a roller coaster ride, but I thought if I left, he would never be saved. At one point I did take a trip with my toddler son to go off and seek the Lord as to what to do. I got so tired of trying to get my husband to be a part of church. I would see the families going to church together, the couples who taught Bible classes together, and I was always alone. I cried out to God for a Christian family. I thought perhaps things would change if I could only have more children, but that possibility had been taken away because of my health.

God had mercy on me. In spite of all the precautions and the obstacles, I became pregnant with a second child. The doctor told me the only case study he had with someone who had the same condition, the pregnancy was fatal. He wanted me to abort the child. I went out of the office in a daze. Why would God, against all odds, allow me to become pregnant again, if it was only to be aborted or cost me my life? My young son needed me, did I really want to take the risk of not being there to raise him? I cried out to the Lord over that weekend. I was supposed to go back with my decision. As I prayed, the Lord spoke to me and told me the child was a blessing He was sending me, and to trust Him, for He would heal me in the midst of the pregnancy. What joy flooded my soul as the Lord spoke these reassuring words to me. But would my husband or my doctor believe me? My husband told me to do what I thought was best. So, I went to the doctor and told him God had spoken to me, and I told him what God had said. He sat silent for a few minutes and then told me he was a believer as well. He said he had never heard God's voice, but he couldn't deny that God could speak if He chose to. He told me he did not want to go against God, so he proposed this to me: we would wait and see. If I began to get worse, he would intervene, but if truly God had spoken, I would get better. He wanted to give the life I was carrying a chance. I agreed with him. I didn't know a whole lot about faith, but I had an inner peace about it all. In a way, this was my first real test of faith and obedience. I was learning to hear His voice and to trust Him.

During the pregnancy they monitored me very carefully. Much to the doctors amazement, I got stronger every day. Even the symptoms of shortness of breath and dizziness disappeared. My heart sounded strong. It was an easy pregnancy, not like my first. I was hoping for a girl. I was going to name her Christie Ann. When the delivery day arrived, they had a cardiologist present, just in case the stress of the delivery proved to be too much, but it was a quick, easy delivery with no complications whatsoever. I have been checked throughout the years, and the condition has never returned, praise God! He had healed me just as He said He would. My second son, Christian, was born, and he was truly a blessing. He was a peaceful child from the moment he was born, sent from God, with a special purpose.

Things seemed to improve with the birth of Christian. My son, Chad, seemed to be delighted to have a little brother. I have to admit that I thought perhaps now that I had given my husband two sons, he might finally love me for real. I still had a problem with rejection and insecurity. I had learned to love the Lord with my whole heart, and I loved my family, but I still had a hard time loving myself. I have to say while I wasn't really in love with my husband, I did love him and was very concerned about his soul being right with God. My husband had taken a job where he was home every day, rather than being gone on the road, so things seemed more peaceful. I was very active at church, and on rare occasion I would convince him to go along, but he never seemed interested in the things of God. I thought perhaps God would use me to "save" my husband. What I didn't realize is that's God's job, not ours. I'm not saying God doesn't use people, He does, but only God can save someone's soul. I think he resented the fact that I wasn't fun anymore. Everything was always so serious with me. My life was my kids, my faith, and I think he felt he didn't fit in. The truth is, we were living in the same house, but on two separate paths.

Still, life wasn't so bad. I was very busy with my kids, and loved being a mom. My parents had moved to Florida, much closer to us. I had friends at church, and the Holy Spirit had given me a peace and a understanding of the Word of God which I did not have previously. Then one day, out of the blue, my husband came home and said he wanted to move to Louisiana (a friend had moved there and told him there was a lot of opportunity there). I cried, I argued, but most of all I prayed. We didn't have a close relationship, and finally I had family and friends, and now he wanted to uproot us and take us where I didn't know anyone. Perhaps he thought if he got me away from all that our marriage might work out. Maybe we could find something in common if we just had the time to be alone. I don't know what he was thinking, but I didn't like the idea in the least. I had substituted my marriage, or the lack of one, with other things, and now he wanted me to go off alone with him. But as I prayed, I kept feeling the Lord telling me to go. It was hard to tell my parents we were going to leave, after they had moved nearer to their grandchildren. But my mother recognized our marriage was not what it should be and thought it was the best thing for me to put my marriage first and follow my husband. Reluctantly, they accepted our decision. It was so hard leaving them again, and it was something I really didn't want to do, yet I had a peace that God was leading me.

I believe I would never have found the strength to follow the leading of God had I not had the experience of being filled with the Holy Spirit. He gave me courage, the power, to take a step out of the security of the comfort range I was in. Small changes were beginning to appear in my life, and with it, more self confidence than I had before. A work was beginning from within, but the Lord needed to take me to a place where I could receive more teaching, more of His Word, in order to set me totally free.

CHAPTER FIVE
"A Move in the Right Direction"

When we arrived in Lafayette, Louisiana, we looked for a place to rent. Again I prayed. The first place we went to was perfect. We took it right away. The owner told me his son lived next door, if we needed anything. I met the son and his wife the next day. I had noticed there was a church down the street, so I asked them what kind of a church it was. They told me it was a Catholic church and asked me if I was a Christian. When I said yes, they began to praise the Lord, telling me they had been praying for God to bring them a Christian neighbor. They were members of a full gospel church, where he was attending Bible College classes in the evenings. They had a weekly prayer and Bible study in their home, which they invited me to attend. I was delighted God had led me to a place where there were Christians right next door.

I went that Friday night to their prayer meeting. To this point, I had never been in a Spirit filled service. It was a shock to say the least. These people were singing and raising their hands, something I had never seen before. Then when they prayed, I heard some praying in another language. It made me uncomfortable, to tell you the truth. I started worrying that perhaps I had fallen into some cult. My first instinct was to leave, but the Holy Spirit spoke to my heart, telling me I should be patient and judge according to the message they would preach. I knew they would not confess Jesus Christ as Lord or talk about the power of the blood of Jesus, if they were some demonic cult, so I decided to calm myself and wait to hear the message. Well, wouldn't you know, the message was about the power of the blood of Jesus! Everything they said lined up with the Word of God, and besides that, they were such loving kind people. We stood and talked a long while after the service. They asked me if I had been filled with the Holy Spirit, and I told them my experience, but I only had it happen once. I didn't know people spoke in tongues, especially in front of others. I was a bit confused, but they began day by day to teach me the deeper things in the Word of God. The Lord had placed these two wonderful people, Ron and Jean Breaux, in my life to instruct me, and I will be forever grateful for their love and patience.

I still had my doubts about whether the experience I had speaking in that other language (or other people doing so) was really from God, or if it was just my mind making it up. One day, while I was praising the Lord, I felt His presence strongly over me. I suddenly began singing this lovely melody in another language. It sounded so beautiful and no one was around, so I just kept singing. I wasn't sure what it was, or why I began singing like that, but it just seemed to flow out of me. Several days later while I was washing the dishes with the television on, I heard the same song. I stopped and went over to the TV. On the news, the President was meeting with the President of Israel, and there was a ceremony at their introduction. I heard the song I had been singing days before. It was the Israeli national anthem! From that point on, I never doubted that it was truly the Spirit of God and not my imagination. Over the next year and a half I learned about healing, about the gifts and ministry of the Spirit, about deliverance and Spiritual warfare. It was as if I was in Bible college. Ron and Jean poured the Word of God into me, and I began to grow in leaps and bounds.

God began to speak to me more and more. On several occasions the Lord would show me a vision of something, and then several days later it would happen just like He had showed me. I wasn't quite sure what His purpose was for me, but I fell more and more in love with Jesus. The relationship in my marriage wasn't as important to me anymore. I would try to take my husband to church, but he wasn't comfortable with the new church I was going to or with my friends who were so on fire for God. He began to drive long distance truck runs, so I was mostly at home with my children and my God. Jesus became my husband, my friend, my parent. Every day with Him got sweeter.

One day I asked the Lord what His call in my life was. He told me to go to Jeremiah chapter one. I couldn't believe the words I read, when God told Jeremiah he was called as a prophet. I thought I must not be understanding the message. I couldn't believe He would call someone who had always been so afraid of rejection to a ministry which has so much rejection involved in it. I dismissed it as my not understanding and told no one. A few weeks later in our Bible study, God gave me a word through Brother Ron. The word was that God had called me to a prophetic ministry. Brother Ron stopped suddenly as if he was surprised with the words he had just spoken to me. He asked me, "Did you know this?" I nodded my head yes and told him God had given the same word to me a few weeks before, but I couldn't believe God really meant ME. I had such an issue with inferiority and fear all my life, it was a hard thing for me to accept. I had hoped He would have given me a ministry to pray for the sick, or teach children, but this seemed so difficult, carrying so much responsibility. Who was I to be a messenger for Him?

I struggled with this calling for a long while. I kept telling God I wasn't worthy to be his messenger. I would think on my past, on my sins, and I felt so unworthy. One evening while I was giving all my excuses as to why I was too unworthy, God spoke to me. He said, "So you think you are not worthy to allow Me to speak through you?" Finally I thought I had gotten my point across. But then God said, "But you think yourself worthy enough to tell Me no, don't you?"

41

It hit me like a ton of bricks. I had not realized what I was doing! I was denying God the right to use me with the excuse I wasn't good enough. Who is? God chooses as He wills, and who are we to tell Him no? I apologized to Him right then and there and repented of my attitude. I told Him from that point on whatever He wanted, whenever, I was His servant and I would no longer deny Him the right to use me in any way He saw fit.

Months went by and God kept showing me things. I became more confident in the leading of the Spirit and in the visions and words He gave me. I began to share these words with Ron and Jean, and God began to use me in giving words of personal prophecy to people. Then one day in the service in the main church (which had close to a thousand members), the Spirit of God moved upon me to bring a word to His people. I felt as if I would faint. My heart was pounding; His word was ringing in my ears. I kept asking Him to confirm the word, and if He wanted ME to speak it out. I was so scared to make a mistake. At the very moment I was asking Him to confirm it to me, a person spoke out in tongues. When they were done, it was silent for a moment, and my mouth opened and the interpretation boomed out. It was more powerful than anything which had ever happened to me. When the message ended, I collapsed in the seat, trembling all over. Many came to tell me what a blessing it was, and how they felt the presence of the Lord. And so, God began to move more and more in my life. It was one of the scariest moments in my life, but I had jumped the hurdle; I spoke out publicly for the first time!

CHAPTER SIX
"The Great Trial"

The Bible states, "To whom much is given, much is required". It also says, "Many are the trials and afflictions of the righteous, but the Lord delivers him out of them all." My growth had been amazing during the first year we moved to Lafayette. I had learned so much in that short period of time. God was moving in my life. My faith had grown, and was soon going to be tested. God was about to turn my world upside down, and test my faith to the extreme.

My days were spent with taking care of my two little sons, reading the Word of God, going to church, tending my garden, and being a home-maker. I saw less and less of my husband as he was running long distance trips to California. I found it easier to live my life with my Jesus and my kids than to live as a wife. I was actually glad for the alone time, not an ideal way to feel about your marriage, that's for sure. I loved to talk about God, but when my husband was home, it was the one thing he didn't want to hear about. I remember pleading with God to change our marriage. I thought perhaps if we would re-dedicate our marriage to the Lord, things might change. I asked Ron if he would be willing to do such a ceremony. He told me only if both of us wanted to do that. I remember asking my husband, but he thought the whole idea was ridiculous. I tried to convince him that our marriage was a disaster and maybe if we had it blessed, things could get better, but he refused to do it. I cried and asked God what more could I do. I had been married nearly seven years, and everything I tried hadn't worked. I felt I was doomed to an unhappy marriage, but I stayed because I felt it was the only way my husband would be saved, and because I had two small children, and no way to support them. I always hoped one day God would change things. But to my surprise, God's reply to my question of "Why won't You bless my marriage?", was: "How can I bless what is not My will?" The situation became totally hopeless to me. I realized I had married this man without God's permission. It wasn't His will for my life, and He doesn't change his will. What made things more difficult was the fact that Ron and Jean were going to be moving to Alexandria to pastor a church there. I had become so dependent upon them. They were my teachers, my friends, my family, and now they were leaving!

In January of 1979 they held a final meeting before their move. Many people came that night, among them was a man who had not been to any of our meetings before. At the end of the service he approached me to tell me the Lord had given him a word for me. He told me God said, "All things come to an end; when they do, don't look back; you will be married again and have more children." I was taken back by this word, and since I didn't know the man, I was a little wary of it. I spoke to Ron and Jean about it the next day, but all they could tell me was this man was a member of the church, but they didn't know much about him either. They cautioned me to leave this word in God's hands and not to put too much stock into it. I sure was going to miss their wisdom and guidance! I had been their disciple, but now God was going to separate me to see if I could stand on my own with just Him to uphold me. It was a difficult time, but it caused me to go even deeper in my relationship with the Lord. Instead of running to them for answers, I had to really seek God and run to Him for answers.

As I spent hours in prayer with the Lord, He gave me a word that took me by surprise. He said on June 28 I would have a new birth in my life, a new beginning. He also told me I would have a daughter and name her Sharon. I was surprised at this word, and wondered if it was really the Lord, or perhaps the influence of what the man had told me. I had wanted more children, especially a daughter, but my marriage was falling apart, and my husband had taken measures so he could not father any more children after Christian was born. What did all of this mean? I was confused as to what I was to do about it. At first I put the two things together and thought I might be pregnant, but that turned out not to be true, so I just dismissed the whole thing as wishful thinking on my part.

A new family from the church rented the Breaux's house. They were a Puertorican family I had seen at church, Ivan and Eileen Diaz. I didn't know them very well but they were very nice, and I was glad to have Christians next door. They told me they had no idea why God told them to move there, as it was further away from Ivan's job, but they felt God wanted them there for some reason. They were only there a couple of months when an old friend of theirs arrived at their doorstep from Puerto Rico.

I will never forget that day. Eileen was standing outside talking to a man when she motioned for me to come over. She introduced this man as an old childhood friend of theirs from Puerto Rico. His name was Sergio Ramirez. I said hello and we stood and talked a few minutes. In those few minutes this man, who was obviously not a Christian, began using vulgar language in telling us a story about his having been in the Navy. I was extremely uncomfortable, so I excused myself and headed across the yard to my house. I remember on the way thinking, "I wouldn't let such a loser stay at my house", to which, God spoke to me immediately and told me to pray for that man. I remember asking God, "What would you want with a man like that?" (Oh how judgmental we can be at times!) God repeated for me to pray for him, so I did. Later on, Eileen apologized to me for his behavior and explained that he was a dear friend whom alcohol had destroyed. His wife and children left him, and his family had rejected him and sent him with a one way ticket to the United States. They were just trying to help him. I was glad I prayed for him like God had asked me to do. To my great surprise, just four days later on Sunday, at church, I saw this man at the altar, with his hands raised to God, accept Jesus into his heart. I was so excited, seeing God answering my prayer so quickly. He started going to the church every time there was a service. I had never seen someone change so drastically before. He was totally delivered from his alcohol addiction.

At the time, the church I was attending was teaching a great deal about faith. This church had services almost every night. They also had a Bible institute. There were many miracles of healing and deliverance on a regular basis. The Spirit of God moved in that place. There were many prophetic messages, and people would dance and worship the Lord. It was a great blessing, and I learned a lot there, but at one point, they began to take it to an extreme as many did in the late 70's. They began to teach that going to a doctor or hospital wasn't an act of faith. There were several families who started having their babies at home, an some tragedies occurred. I struggled with this doctrine. The Jesus I had come to know was loving and merciful. I knew God could heal us but I just couldn't agree with their belief that going to a doctor was a sin. In the midst of my searching God on this and some other issues that arose in the church, I was thrust into the trial of my life.

My son, Christian, was two years old. He woke up one morning with a little sniffle, which I didn't take too seriously. I prayed for him that morning, and the Lord spoke a word to me: "Your son is like a tree planted by the river, who's leaf will never fade; he will produce much fruit in My kingdom." I remember thanking the Lord for this word for my son, but I didn't know why He spoke it to me at that moment. By noon, Christian was running a little fever. Still, I was not too concerned. I prayed for him, gave him some fluids and laid him down for his nap. When I checked on him an hour or so later, he was burning up. I tried to wake him, but he didn't want to wake up. I called a friend who was a nurse. She told me to take him to her doctor's office immediately. I carried his limp, pale little body to the car, and my neighbor Eileen took my older son, Chad, to her house. At the doctor's office, they ushered me directly into a room. They found Christian's temperature was over 104 and gave him an alcohol bath to bring it down, but still he didn't wake up. I was told to take him to the hospital emergency room immediately. I kept praying all the way there. My son laid on the seat next to me, pale and unresponsive. Upon arrival, they took him into a room and began to work on him. They didn't seem too alarmed, so it calmed my fears.

About an hour after I arrived, a doctor came to me and told me these words: "Do you have family here? You need to call them. Your son has Spinal Meningitis and won't make it through the night." I could hardly believe my ears! Was it possible I heard him right? My head was spinning. I felt like someone had hit me over the head with a ton of bricks. Then I heard the same small voice I had heard in the morning, repeating the same message: "Your son is like a tree planted by the river, who's leaf will never fade: he will produce much fruit in My kingdom." Suddenly, I knew why God had spoken that word to me in the morning. I had a choice to make, to believe what the doctor just told me or to believe what God had told me earlier. I chose to trust God. I told the doctor, "That isn't possible; God is going to use my son." He told me he admired my faith, but continued to repeat his diagnosis. He said my son had viral Spinal Meningitis, not the bacterial version, and there was nothing that they could do for him. He said he did not expect him to survive the night, and if he by chance did, he would be severely affected. He would suffer brain damage, perhaps not be able to walk, talk, or speak, in short words, he said my son could be a vegetable for life. I insisted God would do a miracle. When he found he could not convince me otherwise, he advised me again to call my family, and left. I didn't know how God was going to do it, or when, but my faith didn't waver. God would perform a miracle.

They let me go into the the room with Christian after some further tests, and they allowed Ivan and one of the pastors from the church to go in to pray for him. He was in a coma, still unresponsive. We stood around him and began to pray. As we laid hands on him in prayer, it was as if a jolt of electricity went through his little body, and his eyes opened. The nurse, who was present, ran out of the room to get the doctor. He was conscious once again, thank God. His little eyes looked up at me, and I knew he recognized me. Still fever was raging in his body, and he would slip in and out of consciousness, but at least it was a sign that God was doing something.

I called my mother and father. I believed God was going to heal my son, but I also knew I needed my parents to come and help me take care of Chad. I was not able to reach Christian's father, but I did let his company know how urgent it was and they told me they would try to track him down on the road and have him call me. When my husband finally called the hospital, I informed him of what the doctor had said, and what God had told me. His question took me by surprise; he asked if I thought he should come home or not. Perhaps he was in shock, I don't know, but I was so taken back by his response. I think that was the last straw for me. My answer was, "what do you think?" and I hung up.

The night passed with me at Christian's bedside. The next day my parents arrived and stayed with my son Chad. It was a relief to have them there. My husband arrived too. He was upset with me, blaming me and my faith. He thought I had let Christian sick for days without taking him to be checked. The doctor assured him that this illness comes on suddenly and that there was nothing I had done wrong, but he still seemed upset with me. It was a hard time for us all. God had given him a warning through Brother Ron months before telling him to repent and turn to God or there would be consequences. I guess he was angry with God, perhaps with himself, for not heeding the warning. At that point, I didn't really care; all that mattered was my son.

Christian spent the next day in intensive care, still battling the virus in his system. The doctors were amazed he made it through each day. On the second night of watching his suffering, I cried out to God. I knew God would heal him, but I didn't know exactly when it would happen, and watching him suffer was more than I could endure. God spoke these words to my heart: "On the third day My Son arose; on the third day I will raise up your son."

On the third day my mother came to the hospital to stay with Christian and insisted I go home to bathe, eat, and rest. I was hesitant to leave, but she can be pretty convincing, and Christian was sleeping, so I left for a couple of hours. I spent some time with my son Chad, and got cleaned up, but I couldn't rest. I had sent a message to my dear friends, Ron and Jean Breaux, about Christian's condition the day he became ill, but I had not heard from them. I had hoped they would have come to pray for him, and to be with me, but I had heard no response. I left the hospital around 1:30pm. Around 3:00pm my mother came in through the door at home and told me my husband had gone to the hospital and said he would stay for awhile. I quickly got ready and returned to the hospital around 4:00pm. To my amazement, my son sat up and smiled at me. I called the nurse. His fever was indeed gone. I asked what had happened. She told me his father was there for a few minutes and then left. Then two people came saying they were ministers and asked if they could see him. They were only there a short while, around 3:00pm, and then they left. The description matched Ron and Jean. (I spoke with them later and they told me they wanted to leave and come down the very first day they got the message, but God told them to wait until the third day. Isn't that amazing?)

My little boy was now able to sit up and eat. He was totally responsive. They still had him hooked up to IV's and he was restless to get down out of bed and play. The next day after extended tests, they disconnected him and let him get up and walk. The doctor's

49

were amazed. After discussing his case and looking over his records repeatedly, the doctor came to me and asked how I knew ahead of time. They had all the evidence in front of them, and the diagnosis, yet there was no other explanation, but a miracle had occurred. I told him how God had spoken to me the day my son became ill, and that was how I knew there would be a miracle. He said he just couldn't explain it any other way. God had healed my son! He had no defects, no limitations, it was as if it had never happened. Because viral Spinal Meningitis is contagious, by law Christian had to stay for fourteen days, so I spent the next few days ministering to other sick children in the hospital while Christian played. There was a very sick young boy with Leukemia who was so weak he couldn't get out of bed. After prayer, he became so energetic, he pulled the IV's out and was running and playing. He said he felt great, and when they tried to put him back in bed, he locked himself in a bathroom. When they finally convinced him to come out and ran tests on him, they were amazed that his blood cell count had changed drastically. They said he was in remission. Praise God for the miracles I saw. Some of the nurses would join with me at night to pray for the children on the ward. It was an amazing time.

When I was allowed to take Christian home, one of the first things I did was testify at church of all the amazing things the Lord had done. I told them how the Lord had used me to pray for other children at the hospital. The wonderful thing is that many realized how God used the situation to be a blessing to others. There were those who taught going to doctor's or hospitals wasn't of faith, but this testimony seemed to open their eyes. God is everywhere, in everything, and can perform His miracles, through medicine, through doctors, through any one!

After testifying that Sunday, Sergio came to talk with me after the service. He was so excited. It was the first miracle he had ever seen. He said he saw me carrying my son to the car on the day he became ill. He thought he was dead. He told me that same evening when Ivan came back from the hospital, he was crying. He thought Ivan was going to tell them Christian had died, but to his amazement Ivan said, "God is so good". He told them how God had woken Christian from the coma as we prayed. The testimony of his healing greatly affected Sergio's new-found faith. It was a giant bolt to my faith as well. I was so grateful, so in love with my Jesus, who spared my son, and who spared me. I shared the story with anyone who would stand still and listen. God opened many doors for me to minister through this miracle.

CHAPTER SEVEN
"A New Beginning"

As one door shuts, God opens another. I decided to separate from my husband. I had prayed, before Christian became ill, and the events of his illness just seemed to confirm to me that we were not meant to be together. The last thing I had in my mind was finding another husband. I had been married to a man who didn't want anything to do with my faith, and I had learned to make God my husband, my family. Jesus was everything to me. Then I had this dream: I saw the man who had come to see my neighbors, Sergio Ramirez, standing and preaching in a large auditorium. At the end of preaching, he invited people to come for prayer. He began to pray for the people, but at one point, he looked up and saw the line was quite long, so he said, "I need my wife to come and help me pray." I saw myself, in the dream, get up and go stand next to him. I began to pray for an elderly woman who was standing in line. I woke up immediately from the dream. I was completely taken back by this dream. I remember asking the Lord what this all meant, and if this was a dream from Him or not. God replied: "It is", to which I replied, "but how can this be, Lord? I am not looking for a husband, and I am not interested in this man at all." God responded these words, which I will never forget: "In my time, I will put my love in your heart for him, and in his heart for you, and though you are not perfect, the love which you shall have for each other will be, because it comes from Me." My response was, "be it done unto me according to your will." As the days passed, I began to wonder if it had all been a dream. I focused on God and on my children, and tried not to think too much about it. I wasn't attracted to this person at all. I was sure if the dream was from God it wasn't for the present, but for a long time away, or so I thought.

Sergio had taken a job and moved out from the house next door. Still, he came to visit on a few occasions. He worked nearby, so he would walk over to see Ivan and ride to church with him on service nights. One night he arrived, but Ivan had an appointment and didn't come home after work. Sergio came to my door and asked if I was going to church that night, as he needed a ride, since he hadn't purchased a car yet. I told him I would be glad to take him to church, but I had to feed the children and get ready. He invited me to get a quick bite on the way to church. On the trip there, I remember asking him about his ex-wife and children in Puerto Rico. I told him God could restore his family to him. He had tried to minister to his ex-wife by phone, but she just laughed at him. He told me he had been a bad husband, with alcohol ruining everything. We began talking about the Word of God. He had so many questions. He was like a sponge, absorbing everything he could learn. Several days later when he visited his friends again, we stood and talked for over an hour about the things of God. He would come after work to catch a ride to his home with Ivan or to go to church. He would play with all of our kids, and they loved him. Still, I didn't see him as anything but a brother in Christ.

One afternoon, while I was doing some sewing, God spoke to me and told me to get up and go to the store. I couldn't imagine why, as I didn't need anything. I knew it was the store where Sergio was working. I debated over it for a few minutes, but the Lord repeated the message, so I got the boys ready and headed to the store. I thought perhaps there was someone I needed to minister to, so I put the boys in a cart and started walking through the store, looking for why God sent me there. My oldest son, Chad, said he needed to use the bathroom, so I headed to the back of the store where the bathrooms were. As I approached the bathroom, Sergio exited the bathroom. He looked at me rather strangely. I remember I said hello, but he kept staring at me. He looked very pale, and then suddenly he excused himself and went back into the bathroom. I remember thinking he must have a stomach virus or something. God must have had a good laugh that day. I continued through the store and left after I felt a peace about it, not having any idea as to why God sent me there in the first place. The other side of the story I heard later: Sergio had a new life in Christ, he had a job, and everything was brand new for him, but he was lonely. He had asked God for a family. He was reading the Bible on his break and saw a scripture which states, "Ask Me concerning things to come, and concerning the work of My hands, command ye Me." He was so young in faith, even though he didn't understand it, he took it by faith, so he went to the bathroom to pray and ask God to show him who his wife was to be. After praying, he stepped out of the bathroom and there I was standing with my two children right in front of the door! He says he stood there thinking, "but God, that's the lady from next door to Ivan". He was going through this mental debate with God, and I thought he was sick! At any rate, he finally excused himself and went back into the bathroom to tell God, "I think you misunderstood me, God", to which God showed him that he had asked to see his wife, and God had brought me there. What more did he want, for God to put me inside the bathroom? Sergio said he fell flat on the floor and asked God to forgive him. He said he knew from that moment on that I was the one God had chosen for him.

Now, I was completely unaware at the time, what was going on inside that bathroom. God had now confirmed to us both, but neither of us had feelings for each other yet, and didn't dare tell anyone, let alone each other. Over the next few weeks, we continued to converse about the Bible. Sergio asked if it was alright for him to call when he had questions. We would spend hours on the phone studying the scriptures together. He told me his brother was coming from Puerto Rico. His brother also had a drinking problem, and he hoped that all of us could minister to him. I spoke with Ivan and Eileen and we planned a cook out and invited several friends from church. I had not seen Sergio in a few days, as he was busy with his brother and had not come by to see Ivan. On the night of the cook out, he introduced me to his brother. We had more people than I had expected, so I went to the shed to get some more lawn chairs out. He came to help me. Why I said what I said next, I'll never know. I didn't plan to say anything; I wasn't thinking it, but it just blurted out anyway, I told him I had missed him. I couldn't believe I said it. It was so unlike me. To my surprise, he said he had missed seeing me and talking to me too. We both stood there a little awkward for a moment, and then joined the others.

After dinner, the group left to go to a church roller skating activity. Now, I have to say, I can't skate! I have weak ankles. In fact, my only experience in trying to skate or rather ice skate, was when I was in my teens, and it was disastrous. I was there for four hours and spent 3 ½ hours on the ground, and a half hour trying to get back up again! I stopped trying when I fell so hard I chipped my tail bone. So my first reaction to going to a skating party was, NO WAY! But I saw they were all going to go, and I wanted to spend more time with Sergio, so I went along, with the intention of just watching them. Once we were at the skating rink, everyone tried to encourage me to try, but I stayed safely on the side lines. Chad and Christian had on kiddie skates and seemed to be having great fun with the other children. At one point, Ivan and Sergio came and told me they would get me skates that were tightened so the wheels wouldn't roll much, and they promised to hold my hands so I wouldn't fall. Would you believe, I decided to do it just to be able to hold hands with Sergio? I couldn't believe I was acting like such a kid! But, I did it. We went around the ring slowly for a few times. I almost fell a couple of times, but they held me up. Then they announced the last skate was for couples only, girls choice. I wanted to stay with Sergio, but I thought it might look bad if I asked him. While I pondered what to do, a friend, Lourdes, came over and asked Sergio to skate with her. I went and sat down and took off my skates. I remember feeling very foolish, and very annoyed that Sergio was skating with Lourdes. I remember thinking, "It should be me out there with him." I chastised myself for even thinking such a thing, still, I was delighted when we all left to go home that he sat next to me in the back seat of the car.

The next day, Sergio called to thank me for throwing the cook out to welcome his brother. He wanted to repay me by asking me to join him for lunch, so I met him for lunch the next day. We had an unusual conversation, with each of us trying to "fish" for some sign of any evidence of interest on the others part. I thought it was all in my head. I was so afraid of getting hurt, of getting involved in anything that might not be God's will, or God's time. I kept thinking he was just being nice to me because he felt sorry for me being alone with two small sons. I remembered the dream, but I wasn't sure if God meant now, or if it wasn't just me making it all up. He, on the other hand, had the bathroom experience, but being young in the Lord, he wasn't sure if he had gotten it right or not either. It was a very odd conversation. Still, I have to admit, suddenly I felt different when he was around. My heart raced; I couldn't catch my breath. I wondered if I was just being foolish. I had gotten to a point in my life that I no longer believed you could feel like that, or you could fall in love and live happily ever after. It was all just a fairytale. But then I had all these feelings that made me feel like a teenager again. I had to keep telling myself to grow up, I was 27 years old with two kids. I noticed how he would just stare at me and smile. I wondered what he was thinking, did he feel the same feeling? I didn't have to wait long.

One day he called to ask me about something he read in the Bible. While we were talking, in the middle of a sentence, he blurted out, "I think I'm falling in love with you." I froze. I just sat there on the other end of the phone dazed, not knowing what to say. Did I really hear what I just thought I heard? It was too good to be true! Not hearing a response from me, he suddenly began to apologize; he was sorry if he had offended me, to which I answered, "no, no, please….tell me again." Suddenly, it all spilled out, the experience he had in the bathroom when God spoke to him, the dream I had earlier. We shared what God had told us both, and we knew, it was meant to be.

The first thing we did in starting our new family was to kneel down and pray together. We dedicated our relationship, our family, and ourselves to Jesus Christ. We asked the Lord to be the center of our home, the priority of our hearts and lives. We entered a covenant with God to be true and faithful to him and to each other. That was the moment our lifetime together truly began; it was a spontaneous moment, from the heart, before God. The vows we said later before a judge were only the legal formality, but the vows we said that day before God were the true beginning of it all. By the way, the date we prayed and made the commitment to God and each other was June the 28. It was the day God told me months earlier, before I even met Sergio, that a new beginning, a new birth, would happen in my life. We didn't plan to make that commitment in prayer. It happened by the leading of the Spirit of God. Only later did I realize what the date was, and it blew my mind. I realized then what God was trying to tell me before. On the date my divorce became final, we went immediately to the Justice of the Peace and finalized our union by the law of the land.

There are so many wonderful things that happened in those early days. Chad was six, and Christian was two and an half years old. Their father had been gone a great deal of the time, working on the road, so they both welcomed having a man's attention on a daily basis. Sergio would play with them for hours. There were great games of hide and seek, of cowboys and indians, but best of all were the Leggo building events. While Sergio was a strict disciplinarian, too strict at times, but he showed a lot of love and attention to the boys.

When I found out I was pregnant, of course I thought it was the daughter God had promised me. We had an amazing experience regarding this pregnancy. We were visiting my parents in Florida, and on one evening while we were in bed, we both noticed several "light figures" in the room. I counted them and there were four. Sergio saw them as well and counted the same amount. We wondered what it meant. We believed they were angels watching over us. We were sleeping with my two boys in the same room, so we believed it was each of our guardian angels. We stayed there a few weeks visiting, praying for direction, and God led us to take a trip to Puerto Rico. On the night before our flight, the angels were once again visible in our room, but this time there were five "lights". We discussed what this "fifth" light might be, and thought perhaps the Lord had sent an extra angel to watch over us on our trip. Two weeks later we found out I was pregnant, and realized the fifth angel was the baby's guardian angel.

When we arrived in Puerto Rico, I met his family. They loved me from the first moment, and treated my sons as their grandsons. They lived up in a mountain in the rain forest. It was a beautiful, tropical place. I had a very limited remembrance of the Spanish language from my childhood. I remember going out and meeting some of my husband's family and friends. Of course, everyone spoke in Spanish, and I went into cultural shock. I felt so out of place, since I couldn't follow the conversation. I would hear a word here and there that I recognized, but I was really lost. That, and my being emotional because of being pregnant, made the time there a little hard for me.

The rain forest is a wonderful place with rivers and waterfalls. The children loved to explore, and because it was so hot, we often would go to the river so the children could swim and cool off. One day I was sitting on a rock, watching the children play, and I began to pray. All of a sudden, I felt the presence of the Lord. He spoke to my heart a message: "The enemy will try to harm the child within you, but fear not, for I am with you. I have a purpose with this child, and all will be well." I was thankful for the reassurance and knew well how God had warned me beforehand when Christian became ill. I did not know what this announcement meant, but I knew to remain in prayer and to trust the Lord. About two weeks later, I began to have cramps and to bleed. Normally, one would rush off to the doctor, but I remembered what the Lord had said, so Sergio and I prayed the whole day long, while I stayed off my feet. By the next morning the bleeding and cramps stopped, and everything seemed back to normal. I believed by faith that God had healed my baby and me, and the incident did not reoccur. The devil was not able to steal my child or convince me I was miscarrying. The Word of God says, "All things are possible to them that believe", and I believed.

We found an English church and started to attend. It was such a relief to be able to worship the Lord and hear the Word in a language I could fully understand. We were only there a few months, but we had some wonderful experiences at that church. We moved from the mountain to a house owned by Sergio's brother, which was closer to the church. Sergio was working and I was at home with the children during the day. It was a hard time. He had two children from his previous marriage, Liza and Sergio, or Sergito, as we called him. Liza was eight and Sergito was six, like Chad, so they hit it off immediately, even though they didn't speak each others language. Playtime has a language all of it's own. It was great for us to both have our children with us, but economically it was very tough. We struggled to make ends meet. The first Christmas was so tight that we didn't think we would have any presents to give the children. I baked some cookies for Sergio to sell at his place of work, just to help out, but it wasn't enough. Our first Christmas was like something out of the "Charlie Brown Christmas" special. The tree was in a pot, with about ten skinny branches sticking out. We didn't have the money for decorations, but we managed to find a strand of outdoor lights, which we wrapped around the tree. The weight of the lights almost caused the tree to bend. We made decorations out of construction paper to hang on the tree. I took some socks and drew angels on them and stuffed them with newspaper, to make some decorations to place around. It was poor! But we were together and we were happy. On Christmas Eve, Sergio's brother came over in the afternoon and took us to the Army base with him. He was a Vietnam Veteran, who had lost both his legs in Vietnam. He went into the store there and came out with trucks for the boys. My parents had sent me a check that I was able to purchase them a few small toys and some food to make a Christmas dinner. God had seen to it that our kids didn't go without Christmas.

We were invited to a neighborhood Christmas celebration. It was a different experience listening to Christmas songs that didn't sound anything like the Christmas songs I was accustomed to. They roasted a pig in the back yard, and it seemed more like a luau to me than a Christmas party. On the way walking home, my youngest son, Christian, who was almost three, pointed up to the sky and said, "Jesus". We looked up, and didn't see anything but a starlit sky. But he kept saying, "Look, Jesus!" We knew he was seeing something that we weren't able to see. It was the sweetest thing to hear his little voice telling Jesus "I love you, Jesus". We have often mentioned how from such a young age the Lord's call was upon Christian. From God saving him from the Meningitis to this special event, we knew God had something special planned for him. He was such a gentle, sensitive child.

We were very active at church. I went to the women's meetings, and at one meeting, a sister from France came over to me and told me, "you are having a son, and you are to name him David". I thanked her, but inside I didn't receive the word for the child I was carrying, certain that it was the girl God had spoken to me who was to be called Sharon. As much as I liked the church, and was beginning to feel more comfortable in Puerto Rico, economically speaking things did not improve. We felt God was leading us to return to Louisiana, so we left Puerto Rico and returned. I'm not quite sure why God had us go to Puerto Rico in the first place, perhaps it was to meet his family, perhaps it was for him to show them how God had made such a difference in his life. The last time they had seen him, he was a hopeless alcoholic. Now he returned in Christ, eager to win his family to the Lord. We did not accomplish that task in that visit, but the seed was planted. They were able to see with their own eyes the change that had occurred in his life. At the same time, we were able to establish a sense of family with all of our children, something that would last throughout our lifetime.

Sergio & Charlene when they were first married

CHAPTER EIGHT
"Back to where we started"

So now we were back to where we started from, back in Lafayette, Louisiana. The church we had gone to previously had split, and we went with our friends, Ivan and Eileen to the new church which had formed. Sergio got a job working at Burger King as an assistant manager. Eileen's brother worked as a manger there and got Sergio the job. I didn't think it was a good idea, and told him he needed to wait on the Lord, but he felt a job was a job, and we had to start somewhere. Eileen's brother was a great guy, but he was not serving God. The job required Sergio to work nights and weekends, which meant he would miss church a lot. All of these things I felt were not good for someone so young in the Lord. Still, it was his decision. It turned out my concerns were genuine.

Slowly, Sergio was being sucked back into the old self. He began to have an occasional drink with his friend. I knew where this was heading. After several tearful sessions, I realized I was unable to handle it on my own. I was just weeks away from delivering our first child. One night I fell on my face before God and cried. God had set him free, and now Sergio was playing with fire. I prayed for the Lord to show him the truth. He came home that night from work and told me how the Lord had entered the store after they had closed and he was alone doing paperwork. He said the presence of the Lord was so strong, that he had to go on his face on the floor. God spoke to him and told him He had set him free, but his bad choices would lead him to lose me and the family, if he hurt us by returning to his old ways. Sergio said he poured out the drink he had fixed himself right then and there and asked for forgiveness. He came home to wake me up and ask me to forgive him as well. I was so thankful to God for His intervention. The Lord is so faithful. The reason I mentioned this incident was to reflect on how when God sets us free, we still have the old urges and temptations that may arise. God expects us to walk in the new life He has given us, but He doesn't take away our free will to choose which path we will take. Still, when we surrender to temptation and take the wrong path, God is there to lead us back to the right path whenever we repent and call on Him for His help. The scripture says, "Two are better than one, for if they fall, one will help the other up". God hears our prayers when we pray for our loved ones. He will reach out to them in response. It is their choice to respond to Him and accept His help or reject it. I am so thankful Sergio accepted His help. He never returned to take a drink after that.

Several weeks later, I gave birth to our first son, David Daniel. Right there, in the delivery room, in front of the doctor and the nurses, Sergio took our son and held him up before God and prayed. He dedicated our son to the Lord from the moment he was born. He was a fair haired little baby boy, who smiled from the get go. He had a round little face with the cutest dimples and a smile that would light up the day. He was in such a hurry to stand and walk. He never did crawl. At eight months he let go and walked all over the place. He smiled at everyone he met. He brought so much joy and laughter to us all. His older brothers loved him. They would play with him and he would giggle at them for hours.

When David was almost a year old, Sergio had vacation so we decided to go and visit my parents in Florida. When we were about to drive home in our van, my parents gave us a surprise, tickets to Disney World! It was a great day; the boys were so excited. I had never been there either, so it was quite an adventure. We arrived early in the morning with backpacks, filled with snacks, jackets, baby bottles, and diapers, all set to make the most of the day. Not wanting to miss a thing, we stayed until the end to see the electric light parade. It was wonderful. When we finally left, exhausted and hungry, we couldn't find our van. We walked around and around, thinking perhaps we had forgotten where we parked. As the cars slowly all left, we discovered our van had been stolen from the parking lot. In it was our port-a-crib, a cooler with baby milk, diapers, food, clothes, my Bible, and a photo album which we had taken for my parents to see, in short, everything! The Disney Security team helped us check, but to no avail. We had to fill out a stolen vehicle report, and they kindly put us up for the night. We had no car, and only a little money for the trip home. At that time, we didn't own a credit card, and we didn't bring our checkbook, but in truth, it didn't have much of anything in it. We called my parents and they provided us with bus tickets so we could return back to Louisiana. It was a big downer coming off such an awesome day. I don't know why it happened, as it was not a common occurrence at Disney World, but sometimes things happen that you don't understand. God tries your faith in those times. We were determined to praise God regardless of the hardship.

When we returned back home, Sergio lost his job. He had no transportation, so he could no longer continue at the Burger King. He would have to find a job within walking distance of our home. The apartment complex we lived in had an opening for a painter, and for a housekeeper. We took the jobs immediately, and it turned out to be a great blessing. Sergio painted vacant apartments and steam cleaned carpets. He listened to the Christian radio station as he painted. It became his Bible College in a sense. Teaching after teaching were aired all day long. He grew so much as a Christian, and before long, the fire of God was burning once again as it had been in the beginning. He was home nights and weekends, and best of all, we spent all day long together. It didn't pay as well, but we were able to get by. We had no transportation to get to church, or anywhere else for that matter, so we started a home group. We gathered with other Christians in our community to study the Word of God. It was an amazing time.

By the time I became pregnant again, we had grown so much in the Lord, but financially, things were still pretty tough. We were not able to save up enough to buy another car. But God touched the heart of a dear friend from our Bible study group who bought us a car. What a surprise that was! It was a station wagon, big enough to fit all the kids. Liza and Sergito would come to be with us in the summertime, so then we would have five children. What a blessing that sister was to us. Wherever she is, I still pray God continues to bless her for her kindness and generosity towards us.

When I was about seven months pregnant, I kept feeling I was not to have the baby at the hospital. I spoke with Sergio about this, but he was uneasy about us having the baby at home. I had prayed, and God showed me a vision of the birth; I was at home in my room, and when the baby came out, He was there and He caught the baby in His arms at the moment of birth. The Lord told me, "I promise you I will be there." Sergio prayed, and God told him to trust the words He had spoken to me and to not be afraid. There was a pastor's daughter we knew who was a midwife, which we asked to deliver our baby. She prayed and felt it was of the Lord, so she agreed. It was the most amazing experience. On the day I went into labor, October 18, 1982, I had already given birth three previous times, so I knew, or thought I knew, what to expect. All I kept feeling was pressure. I called my midwife, and she came by to check. She told me I would have the baby within hours. Sergio, Alice (the midwife), and our friend Deidre were present. We talked and laughed. It was more like a social gathering than a delivery room. I felt the pressure intensify, but I had no pain. Finally, Alice checked and told me it was time. I remember thinking perhaps she didn't know what she was talking about, as this was nothing like what I remembered from previous births. But sure enough, I gave birth to a nine and half pound baby girl, without any pain! What a joy when she told me it was a girl! Sergio says my face lit up. I had my little Sharon, finally! Sergio prayed and dedicated her to the Lord as he had David.

The boys were all delighted that they had a baby sister. Little David, who was only two, absolutely loved her. He would kiss her every chance he got. What wonderful days those were. Every mother looks back and remembers her most happiest times as being those of when her children were little. My mother told me my grandmother used to say, "when your children are little, your troubles are small; when your children are big, your troubles get bigger". Over the years, I have found that to be a true statement, but the joys of being a parent far out-weigh the struggles and responsibilities.

After Sharon was born, I returned to work, but developed bursitis in my heel. It became almost impossible for me to continue working. I spent six months limping with the pain. I prayed and prayed, but the pain continued for some reason; it was a test I had to endure. At the same time, the manager of the apartment complex left taking another job. The new manager was not like the first. She was a difficult person to work for. Things became harder for us in every aspect. She often would have me do some office work for her, which was a blessing as I could sit and not be on my foot, but on one occasion, she instructed me if the main office called, I was to tell them she was out on the grounds, and she would call them back. I was told to call her pager and let her know, as she wanted to go shopping. I told her very respectfully I was not going to lie. Had she told me she was going on the grounds, and gone elsewhere, I wouldn't have known the difference, but since she told me she was going to the Mall, I would be lying. She knew she would get in trouble for shopping on company time, and she wanted me to cover up for her. I refused to participate, and it infuriated her. She began to curse at me, and when I told her I was very sorry, but I had to answer to Jesus and my conscious first, she in blunt words, told me what I could do with my Jesus and fired me.

Now what were we going to do? We could barely make it with us both working. Sergio was upset, but not with me. He was proud of me for doing the right thing. Still, we didn't know how we would make ends meet. But, the upside was I would not be on my foot all day long. By the time we paid all our bills, it left no money for food, but God did not leave us. One day we found a bag with groceries and an envelope with some money on our front door step which said, "from Jesus". A friend told us of a church in town that gave food to needy families. It took a lot of humbling, but Sergio went to ask for help. The pastor of the church heard him speaking to the secretary, explaining our circumstances. The pastor, Robert King, came from his office and took Sergio to the food room and began to serve him. He put all kinds of things in boxes for our family. Sergio was so impressed by his love and compassion, that when he came home with the great blessing, he told me, "I want to go and hear this man preach." We went to the church that Sunday, First Assembly of God, in Lafayette, Louisiana, and we felt we had come home. Pastor King was the most loving man I had ever met. He was an elderly man, but he would get down on one knee to hug the children, and he was always surrounded by them. He would disappear after service, with a stream of children following him. Soon they would all appear again, with cookies in hand. He kept a cookie jar in his office, and to this day, my children remember him for the hugs and the cookies.

The church was a loving place of about two hundred members. Amazingly, people were very close, even though it was a rather large group. They helped us get back on our feet, and we loved being there every time the doors were open. I asked the Lord why he had sent us there one day, and the Lord told me this: "Pastor King is the best groomer around. Before the horse goes to the race, he goes to trainers, but the very last person the horse sees is the groomer. I have sent you to the best groomer around." Boy, was that true! Pastor King was a pastor's pastor. He was what a pastor should be. He was patient, loving, kind, humble, and devoted to the Lord, and to his sheep. We had all the training in the word, training in the gifts of the Spirit, but this man lived the fruit of the Spirit. We had received instruction and the gifts God had given us in order to minister, but this man was placed in our lives to teach us how to use them in love. What a blessing those days under his ministry were to us. (At the writing of this book, I received news that our dear Brother King went to be with his beloved Jesus, so I wish to make a tribute to him for the great example of Christ he lived before us all.)

We became involved in several outreach ministries through the church. We taught Sunday School, visited nursing homes, and started to go to the prison in Baton Rouge. Sergio had a real gift in ministering to those who were incarcerated. The testimony of how God had delivered him from alcoholism, and the passion he had for Christ, greatly impacted many of the inmates. He had the true heart of an Evangelist. Soon he became part of the team that ministered in the prison. He went to the prison for men once a month, and we went together to the woman's prison once a month. Before long, the director of the ministry to the women left, and he asked us to take over the ministry. We had wonderful experiences at the prison. God saved lives, comforted sisters, healed and blessed so many.

One evening as we were returning from the prison, it seemed as if we had entered a fog. We had to cross a bridge that was about 18 miles long, with no place to stop or turn around, which crossed one of the many Louisiana bayous. Not long after we began to cross the bridge, our car began to act strange, and went off. It was late at night. There were no call boxes (and this was before cellphones). When we got out of the car to check under the hood, we realized that it was not fog, it was smoke coming from our car. As we stood there in the dark, I looked down and noticed a glow, like a light, from under the car. I remember asking Sergio, "Do we have a light that comes on under the car?" He got down and checked, along with another brother who had accompanied us. It was our catalytic converter! It was as red as an electric burner! We all backed away from the car immediately. (For those who may not know, the catalytic converter has gas flowing through it). We were alarmed that the car could blow up! As we all began to pray, one young brother reminded us of the power of God we had seen that night in the prison, and said we should lay hands on the car and pray together in faith.

Encouraged, we overcame our fear and gathered around the car, laying hands on it, and began to pray. We heard a sound like a hiss, like when you put a hot frying pan under water. The light shining from under the car faded away. Sergio looked again, and the converter was no longer red. We prayed some more, and got back into the car. Sergio asked the Lord if it was safe to drive, to let the car start. It started up right away, and we drove across the rest of the bridge. When we reached home, we told our babysitter what had happened. Her boyfriend, who was a mechanic, stopped by to pick her up. When we told him what had happened, he took a flashlight and went and looked under the car. He came out puzzled and amazed at what he saw. He said the catalytic converter looked brand new, and the rubber seals were like new. He told us if the converter had gotten that hot, it should have exploded, or at least, melted all the seals, but this look like a new one that had just been installed! We shared this testimony with everyone at church. What an amazing, miraculous intervention from the Lord!

Another wonderful thing happened in those days when my parents came to visit us and stayed with us for a week. My mother believed in Jesus since she was a young girl, but my father never did. He used to tell me he wished he had faith like I did, but he just didn't believe. I had tried in the past to "preach" the Gospel to him, but it just turned him off even more. When I moved to Lafayette, leaving my parents behind in Florida, one of my biggest concerns was I would not be there to lead my dad to Christ. I remember the Lord spoke to me back then and told me if I would be faithful to serve Him, and just be a "silent" witness to my dad by showing him the love of Christ, rather than telling him about it, God would take care of saving my dad, and my whole family.

While he was there, he and I went out to the store together and had the opportunity to talk. He told me he recognized how important my faith was to me and he wished he could believe like I did, but he just couldn't. He knew how disappointing it had to be that I was not able to "convert" him, but he just didn't believe there was a heaven or hell, or any life after death. Since he brought up the subject, I told him, "Well, either you are correct, or I am, right?" He agreed with me, so I took it a step further. "So if you're right, it doesn't make a difference one way or the other, whether you believe or not." He agreed again. I continued, "But if I'm right, and there is a God, a heaven and hell, then believing in God makes all the difference in the world." He thought for a moment and then responded, "yes, it would make a big difference." At that point, I told him, "Daddy, I love you so much, and if I happen to be right, I just want you to be with me in heaven forever." He sat quietly for a few seconds, and I could see his eyes tearing up. "Is that why you preached at me for so many years?" He asked me. When I told him yes, he became very choked up and just nodded his head. After a few quiet seconds, he changed the subject.

Several days later, one morning Sergio got up early and was praying. The Lord told him to go out to the kitchen and talk to my dad. He found my father sitting at the table drinking a cup of coffee, so he fixed himself a cup of coffee and sat down with him. My dad told Sergio that the conversation he had with me kept stirring in his mind. Sergio talked with him for quite a while and then asked him if he would like to pray and accept Christ into his life, to which my father said yes. He prayed with my father and led him to the Lord right then and there! What a joyful day for me!

CHAPTER NINE
"The training ground"

God was preparing us for greater things, but it sure didn't seem that way to us at the time. We went through so many trials and experiences in the early days, but we always saw the hand of God. One day we had a real scare. Our son David was friendly and outgoing, but he was also quite a clown. On this particular day he decided to play hide and seek from us, which was nothing new, but this time he moved from one place to another. We looked for him, and couldn't find him in his usual hiding spots. We thought perhaps he had gotten outside, so we began to look around the apartment complex for him. When we didn't find him, and no one we spoke to had seen him, we went back to check indoors again. We checked different places than we had checked the first time. What we didn't know is he left the first spot and went to another spot and fell asleep there. When we still didn't find him, we decided to check the woods and the ravine on the outskirts of the complex. We were praying continually, and at one point we decided to split up in order to cover more ground. I remember crying to the Lord, as the fear began to rise in me. The Lord spoke to me and asked me if I really believed He would allow something to happen to David. My mind was racing, and at that point, the Lord told me to answer the question not with my mind, but from my heart. I stopped, closed my eyes, took a deep breath, and looked into my heart; I had seen the hand of God, His faithfulness to our family, and I knew His great love. We had given our child to Him from the very moment he was born, so did I believe God would allow something horrible to happen to him? My heart said, "no". A peace came over me as I stood there on the sidewalk. I felt the voice of the Lord tell me, "go home", so I turned around and walked back home. When I walked into the house, I felt led to go and check behind the sofa again, and there he was, fast asleep.

Then there was the time I took David and Sharon to the park while Chad and Chris were at school. The park had a deep pond that ducks used to come to, and the kids just loved feeding them bread. David was about four by then and Sharon was a toddler. After we finished feeding the ducks, we walked to the nearby playground area. The children were busy playing and running, so I sat down to watch them. Sharon saw a duck and started running after it. I got up to go after her, but she was running down hill towards the pond. She fell and started to roll towards the deep end of this pond. I ran as fast as I could, but she hit the water before I reached her. She was under water when I got there, but I was afraid if I dove in she would sink deeper, so I slid down the side of the pond and reached in and grabbed her out. I could see her little eyes looking up at me from a few inches under the water, but thank God it was a matter of a few seconds, and she hadn't swallowed too much water. I took her home and bathed her, as it was not a very clean pond. When Sergio and the children came home, I told them what had happened. Sergio told me that in the same spot, when Sergito was visiting us, he had fallen in, and said there was a great under current there. Sergito was a good swimmer, and he said he couldn't swim out; it was pulling him down, but Chad had been there and pulled him out. I realized how close I came to losing my little girl that afternoon and thanked the Lord for not letting anything happen to her.

But one of the biggest interventions from God that occurred in those days happened to Sergio. He was at work and a bad storm was approaching. The manager asked him to go and clean out the gutters of each of the buildings. These two story buildings had flat roofs, which could accumulate water rapidly if the gutters were clogged. He started out early in the morning climbing up on the roof to clean out the gutters. The storm was due to arrive in the afternoon. Sometime after noon the clouds began to roll in. As the afternoon wore on, the clouds became darker and darker, and the winds picked up. Sergio was on the last of the thirteen buildings, hurrying to get finished before the rains began. He said he felt a little concerned as the sky was so black. He began to pray that the Lord would help him finish the job in time. A scripture crossed his mind, and he opened his mouth and spoke it out, "though you pass through the waters, they will not overcome you; though you pass through the fire, it will not kindle upon you, for I am with you." He was comforted with these words and tried to finish the job quickly and get off the roof. Suddenly, a lightening bolt hit him! He fell face down onto a wet roof. He said it was as if someone had taken a two by four block of wood and hit him on the top of his head. His knees buckled underneath him and he fell flat on his face. When he got over the stun, he managed to get up. He took his cap off to look at it, but it didn't seem to show any damage. He began to climb down the ladder and noticed that one foot was hurting him. He limped home to tell me what had happened.

He told me the story and sat down to remove his shoe and check his foot. To our surprise, his large second toe was black and blue. We sat there wondering if it had really been possible that he was struck by lightening, and thanking God for protecting him. That night at church we told the story. One brother who was in the construction business asked Sergio to remove his shoe so he could see his toe. The evidence was there! The lightening had entered through his head and exited his toe, leaving it black! I remember that evening thanking God for sparing our family as I realized I could have become a widow that day. The Lord spoke to me and told me that many lives depended on Sergio's life. I was very moved and extremely grateful. Once again, my Jesus had miraculously intervened in our lives!

The children grew spiritually at First Assembly as well. We enrolled them in the school there, and they loved it. They were active in Royal Rangers and in the children's church. We would often pray together at home, and on one occasion, on a Saturday night while we were praying, Chad began to pray for a young boy. He said his name was Marcus and he was in the hospital with diabetes and he was shaking real bad. The devil wanted to kill him, he said, and then to our surprise, Chad began to rebuke the devil and pray for this young boy's healing. That Sunday as we sat in church, a visitor stood and asked if she could share a testimony. She said she was the mother of a ten year old son named Marcus. She said he had severe diabetes, and began having violent seizures. She rushed him to the hospital the day before, and that night the seizures were so violent, one after another, that the doctors were afraid they would lose him. Then suddenly, they stopped and he slept the night without them returning. She had to come to church to thank God, and she felt moved to share her testimony with us. I could barely hold back the tears. When she was finished, I raised my hand and asked if I could share a testimony as well. I told the church how God had moved on Chad to pray for a young boy he had never met, and shared what had happened the night before. From that day on, Marcus was well and began to attend our church along with his family. Chad and he became great friends, and he would always say, "this is the guy that saved my life".

One day Chad asked if he could share a message at children's church. He shared how God had healed his brother Christian from meningitis, and talked about having faith in God. We were so proud of him. He and Christian were baptized together at church, and they both did so well in school there that they received the Supervisors award. Christian's teacher awarded it to him for having the most "Christlike" character. Indeed, we were proud of them, and most thankful to God for His hand in their lives. That summer Sergito and Liza came to stay with us and Chad and Sergito went to the Royal Ranger summer camp. While they were there, they were both touched by the Lord and received the Holy Spirit.

We still lived at the apartment complex, and Sergio worked there, but that was all about to change. God was speaking to me more and more. One day, in prayer, God gave me a word for the manager of the apartment complex. It was a loving, but also harsh word. God was giving this woman a chance to repent before there would be consequences for some of her actions. I did not know what things the Lord was referring to, but I was certain it was from the Lord. When Sergio came home, he read it, and also feeling it was from the Lord, told me to give it to her. The following day, she called Sergio into the office and asked him if he was aware of the letter his wife had sent. He said that he was, and it was sent with his approval. He was promptly fired.

The following day a policeman, who was also the security guard for the complex, came to our door to deliver us a formal eviction notice. He told us the manager had called the police and turned the letter over to them, claiming it was a threat. The officer told us he could not see how the letter was anyway threatening, but he had to deliver the eviction notice. We had 48 hours to be off the property! If we were not out, our belongings would be placed on the street! How were we going to find another place to live with four children in such a short time? We had no money for a deposit elsewhere. Most apartment complexes were two bedroom, and they were not allowed to rent to people with over two children. I spent the day calling different places, to no avail. We prayed hard! Finally, an apartment complex in the area had compassion on us and agreed to rent to us, even with four children, and was willing to let us move in with the first month's rent, and we could pay the deposit in installments. We praised the Lord for his provision, and started to pack everything for the move.

It was a Saturday morning, and we were in the process of packing the station wagon and running back and forth in the move. Sergio had just turned off the burner after heating water for coffee. I was packing some things from the cupboard, when little Sharon, not yet two years old, reached her hand up and put her hand on the stove. Her little fingers stuck to the electric burner and she let out a scream. I turned to see what was happening, and quickly pulled her fingers off the burner, but she was severely burned. Sergio ran in and we immediately began to pray. The skin was burned on two of the fingers, and we put some ice on it and continued crying out to God. We had no insurance, we had only a couple of hours left to be out, so what were we suppose to do? In the midst of icing her fingers and praying, the phone rang. Sergio went to answer it. It was his mother calling from Puerto Rico. She was hysterical, crying that his brother had gotten drunk and had gotten into a fight with his other brother. One brother took out a gun and shot attempting to shoot his other brother, but the bullet missed and had hit his father instead. Sergio, the youngest of the three brothers, was the only one in Christ, the only one free from alcoholism. She kept saying, "You have to do something, son, help us." What was he suppose to do? He had no money to go there, our daughter was burned, and we were going to be evicted in hours. He cried out to God; actually he shouted, "God, you have to be God right now, because I can't go any further!" Sharon stopped crying. I took the ice compress off her fingers, and they looked pink. The burn was gone! God had healed our baby girl! We were so thankful to God for this miracle. The Word of God says he will not allow us to be tried above what we are able to endure. We finished the move on time, and settled in at our new apartment. We were scheduled to minister at a nursing home that evening, so we left the boxes unpacked, and went to share the gospel, as scheduled. How could we cancel when God had given us a new refuge, and had healed our baby girl?

The next morning at church, Sergio was still overwhelmed by the recent events, and although grateful for what God had done, he was still very concerned about his family in Puerto Rico. He went to the altar that morning and broke down in tears. As he sobbed, a young man from the church, who was an orphan, came to the altar and put his arms around Sergio and just held him. Sergio told me later it was as if the Lord Himself had held him in His arms and whispered the words, "it will be alright". Two days later he received a call from his mother. The bullet had just grazed his father. His one brother was arrested, but the other did not press charges; the brother who had instigated the whole thing decided to leave the Island and move to Texas. The situation was solved, and she was calling to thank us for our prayers. God had intervened! What a mighty God we serve!

Ramirez family, at First Assembly of God in Lafayette, La,.
(left to right) Sergio with baby Sharon, Charlene,
Chad, David, and Christian

CHAPTER TEN
"God Speaks"

I have found at the end of great trials, a great blessing awaits. It was 1984, and we were in a new home, with Sergio looking for a new job. He was finally able to use his college degree for something, as he landed a job as a group home counselor for the mentally challenged. It was better pay, and things seemed to be looking up. We would get together and pray each day before he left for work, and on one of these mornings, the Lord spoke to me and told me from that point on, He wanted me to write down the things He would tell me. So, the next morning I brought a notebook and a pen to prayer. Just as the Lord had said, He began to dictate a message to me. It was a message to His church. Each day there would be a new message, some were exhortations, some were admonitions. As we would pray, Sergio would see me open the notebook and begin to write, so he would get up quietly and leave the room, keeping the children quiet, as I wrote. Sometimes the words would come so quickly, that I would write nonstop filling pages. When the Lord stopped speaking, I would sit back and read what He had just dictated. The amazing thing is that I learned from these dictations. They did not come from my mind, and they required no thought on my part. It was definitely the Lord writing these messages. Some contained revelations of things or events to come. God had showed me many such things in the past. When He first would show me things, I wondered if it was just my imagination, but God had caused so many of them to come to pass, that over time, I learned to trust they were from the Lord. Now He had me writing them down and dating them.

Before long, I had filled the notebook and had started on another one. We were so blessed by the words the Lord was sending us, but had no idea why He was sending them. I tried to share them with the pastors in the area, but either they didn't believe me, or they were too busy to listen. I gave them to my pastor, who believed the Lord was doing something. There were a few he allowed me to share in the church, but some he felt were too deep for the general congregation to receive. He was cautious, as there were many new Christians in the church that he felt would not understand, but he never discouraged me. He told me that since many were prophetic, only time would tell if they were truly from the Lord, but mostly he felt the Lord was giving me this revelations for us to intercede.

During this first year, Sergio continued to work and I stayed home with the children, and to write. We also had added to our outreach by becoming volunteer chaplains at the local hospital. There was a detox unit for drug and alcohol intervention, and Sergio would go and minister to those who were addicted to alcohol. I often went with him when we had someone to watch the children. We saw such wonderful testimonies of deliverance and salvation, too many to list. We wanted to serve the kingdom of God, and wherever we could take the love of Jesus, we went! We saw many people give their lives to Christ!

We were very active at First Assembly. One evening they had an evangelist come and preach on the Holy Spirit. At the end of the message he invited those who wanted to receive the Holy Spirit to come forward to the altar for prayer. The altars filled with people, and he asked for the elders and ministers to come and help pray for the people. Pastor King motioned to us to go and help at the altar. I was kneeling and praying for a woman there when someone tugged on my sleeve. It was my four year old son, David. I tried to tell him mommy was praying and he needed to go back to his seat and sit down, but he insisted that he wanted to receive the Holy Spirit as well. I told him to kneel at the altar and wait until mommy was done praying for this lady and I would pray with him. I continued to pray for the woman, and the evangelist, seeing what had happened, came over and spoke with my son. The next thing I know, there was my four year old son raising his hands to heaven and receiving the Holy Spirit. He was speaking in tongues! He was so excited! When we got home that night, he jumped out of the car and started running around in the parking lot praising God, jumping and shouting. It was all we could do to get him to quiet down and come in. (It was very late). How blessed we were to see the Lord moving in the lives of our children!

One morning in prayer, God revealed to Sergio how he had always asked God to show us His will, but this particular morning, he felt God telling him to ask Him to "DO HIS WILL". He prayed that way, and then went to work. In the afternoon he returned home to tell me that they had called him into the office to let him know they were downsizing, and his job had ended. He couldn't understand at first, that on the very day God led him to pray that way, he lost his job! Yet, it was obvious to us that God was telling us to trust Him, and that He WAS doing His will. Sergio began to look for other work, but to no avail. It was a trying time. We had to move out of our apartment, because we couldn't pay the rent. What was God doing? Could this possibly be His will? We asked all these questions and more. There was a man in our congregation who owned rental property, who when he heard of our situation, he told us he had an duplex that had a vacancy. He was willing to let us move in and pay as we could. What a blessing!

We had some great experiences in that little townhouse, some of them were rather comical. One day after I had picked up Sharon from the church pre-kinder program, her teacher approached me chuckling because she had asked the children what they wanted to be when they grew up. She said Sharon replied she wanted to be like her mommy and tell others about Jesus and she also wanted to be a "belly dancer". Of course the teacher was a friend of mine from church, and she joked with me that she didn't know I moonlighted as a "belly dancer". What Sharon actually meant was a "ballet dancer".

On another occasion after I picked her up and we were at home having lunch, in the middle of eating, her eyes welled up with tears and she said, "I have to give my life to Jesus right now!" I was a bit taken back, as she was only three years old! I told her we would talk about it more after lunch, but she was insistent; "No, right now!" So I took her little hand and prayed with her. I led her in a prayer to accept Jesus as her savior. What a wonderful privilege for a parent! When we were done, she went back to eating. She told me in the school devotional service that morning the pastor was talking about Jesus coming back when the trumpet sounds and everyone who has asked Him into their hearts would get to go with Him. As we finished our lunch, a car outside honked it's horn. Her eyes got as big as can be and she stated, "Jesus is honking, it's time to go with Him!" After fighting back the laughter, I had to explain to her that it was just a car horn, but assured her one day Jesus would come for us all.

She amazed me with her insight and ability to communicate. She was far more mature than most those who were her age, and she was very interested in the things of God.

God continued to speak to me in those days, but I have to admit, I had gotten a little discouraged. As the days passed, and God revealed more of His messages to me, I began to wonder why He was giving such important messages and revelations to me. I remember telling Him once, "Why don't you tell this to people who are in the position to share them with the world?" I tried sending them to several large ministries, but got back a "Thank you for your interest in our ministry" response. I really thought God had picked the wrong person to give these treasures to. One day in prayer, frustrated, I told Him, "These messages are so important, but I'm a woman, an uneducated, poor homemaker, that nobody wants to listen to. I am a hindrance to you,

Lord." The Lord showed me a vision in response to my prayer: I saw
the earth and a great hand was hovering over it. In the palm of the
hand was a stack of papers. I saw a mouth blow on the pile of papers,
and they began to float like falling leaves to different places all over
the earth. I knew the Lord was telling me that these messages were
in His hands, and He would see to it that they reached where He
wanted them to. Then a Puertorican sister and dear friend, Lourdes
Rodriguez, who often babysat for us when we would go to minister,
told us her father was a deacon of a church in Puerto Rico and he was
very interested in prophetic things. She asked if she could send a copy
of the messages the Lord had given me to him. I was delighted that
someone was interested in reading them, so I gave her copies which
she mailed to him.

Sergio did some odd jobs, as well as some painting for people in
the congregation. I tried getting a job as well. There was little work
available in Lafayette during that time due to the oil crisis in 1985. I
found a part time job stocking candy boxes in places of local business.
I also tried selling a line of cookware, but I was a lousy salesperson.
We would often go out with the kids to collect aluminum cans. It
provided extra money for gas. The church food program and some
government help kept us afloat, but we were barely treading water.
As the year went on, things got worse. We couldn't pay our electric
bill. It was several months behind, and one day, in the coldest time
of the year, we received a notice that our service was going to be
shut off. Sergio and I prayed for God to intervene. The next morning
Sergio went to the electric company and asked if he could speak with
someone. He told them we had four children and he had tried to find
work, but please, not to cut the electricity on us, some how, he would
find a way to pay if they would just be patient. She looked up our case
and informed him that the bill had been paid by an agency named,
SMILE. Sergio asked her what this agency was, and she told him she
had no idea, they had never heard of it before. He came home to tell
me, almost in tears, that the Lord had paid our bill!

We were grateful to the Lord for these blessings, but the trial continued. It was as if God was seeing just how much we could handle. When it got too bad, He would step in miraculously, but then the struggle would return. It was if there was no end to the struggle in sight. How could this be happening when all we wanted to do was serve the Lord? Sergio couldn't even get a job as a janitor, or counter worker. Things were so tight. I remember crying thinking I was delusional thinking God was speaking important messages to me. The reality was we were almost homeless. I felt so ashamed, like we were such a poor testimony to others. Still, we continued to pray, and God continued to speak. In April of 1986, a strange new thing happened, the messages seemed to taper off some, but at the same time, I began receiving strange dreams. I would see myself preaching to Hispanic people, in Spanish! These dreams continued over several nights. I knew it was Spanish, as I recognized a few words, but other than that, I had no idea what I was saying, other than the fact I was in a church setting, with a microphone in my hand. I remember telling Sergio about these dreams, and we both wondered what it meant. It didn't make sense to me that I was the one preaching, when I wasn't a preacher in English, let alone in Spanish. I wondered why I didn't see Sergio preaching, since he was a preacher, and Spanish was his first language. None of it made much sense to me. Sergio thought perhaps one day God would take us to a Spanish speaking country, and I would learn Spanish and become a preacher. We had no idea what was in store, but we were going to find out sooner than we expected.

We continued to go and minister as we always had, and God continued to use us; it was all so hard to understand, but then, the trying of your faith always is. One evening as I was driving home from trying to sell the cookware unsuccessfully, I broke down in tears. I remember telling the Lord: "Can't you see we are drowning here? If you don't come to our rescue, we aren't going to make it!" But God didn't answer me. He had stopped speaking to me for the first time in a long, long time. I could handle all the trials, but His silence was devastating. I kept wondering what I had done wrong. Everything was wrong. It couldn't be God's fault, so it had to be mine. I would go back and forth between blaming myself, and then being angry at God. Everything we tried to do to help ourselves out of this pit failed. In bitter tears that night, I cried out as if I were truly in perilous waters, and God didn't say a word! I could have just said, "forget it all", at that point, but I didn't. After a few minutes of waiting for the Lord to speak, a few minutes of tears and silence, I made a decision. I told the Lord, "If You never speak to me again, if You do nothing to help me out of this, I am still going to serve You! I am still going to love You, and praise You, and thank You, regardless, for who You are, and for all You have already done for me." I felt a peace after this, and continued home.

In June of 1986, a dear friend and member of the church, Charles Lewis, told Sergio he was feeling a leading to go and preach in Puerto Rico, but he would need Sergio to go with him to translate. It would cost about four hundred dollars for this trip, and we were four months behind on paying the rent, so how could he come up with four hundred dollars for a trip! Still, they prayed in agreement that if the Lord wanted them to go, somehow He would provide. Within a week Charles called to say a very rich woman had called him to ask if he would come and paint a few rooms in her house. She was going to pay him eight hundred dollars for the job. He asked Sergio to come and do it with him, and they would both receive the airfare for the trip. Although we needed the money for so many other things, we couldn't ignore the fact that it was the exact amount they had need of for this trip. They spoke with Lourdes to see if she could contact her father about coordinating some preaching engagements for them in Puerto Rico. He replied he would be delighted to do so, and they were welcome to stay at his house, so they called the airlines. In the meantime, they painted the house, but as the days went by, Sergio kept feeling I was suppose to go with him to Puerto Rico. Now that was impossible! For me to go, the children would have to go too, and that would be a thousand dollars more! Still, we prayed that if this leading was from the Lord, He would provide.

A few days later, a minister came to our church. He was amazing! God used him in the prophetic gifts. He had a word for me. He didn't know me but God showed him things about me, the prophetic call in my life, the trial I was in, and the reassurance that God had called me and would use me for His glory. I was so thankful for this confirmation. I wanted to support this man's ministry. He was greatly used by God, and when they took up the offering for him, a strange thing came to my heart. I had ten dollars left in my purse, which was all we had for the rest of the week, but I felt the Lord leading me to give it in the offering. I remember saying, "Lord, if you want me to go with Sergio and Charles to Puerto Rico, I need a thousand dollars. All I have is this ten, but I am going to give them to your servant, and believe you will multiply it back to me a hundredfold if you want me to go." I told Sergio later that night what I had done. He agreed with me in prayer. No one else knew what I had done, or that we were praying about me going to Puerto Rico. On Tuesday afternoon of that same week, we received a phone call. It was a sister from church who was the music director. She told me she had been up most of the night, as the Lord kept telling her something. She was suppose to give us a thousand dollars for me and the children to go to Puerto Rico with Sergio. I was so overwhelmed, I passed the phone to Sergio, and fell on my knees in tears. The Lord finally spoke to me in that moment. He told me this: "The night you cried out to me that you were drowning, and you thought I didn't hear you, well this is your answer." I was so overjoyed, so thankful to the Lord. God is so faithful. In the midst of the trials, I didn't know it had all been a test, a test of our resolve, our determination, and our faithfulness. God was about to give us a tremendous blessing, but we had to go through the test to see if we would be faithful with what He was about to entrust into our hands. I had no idea even at that moment what it all meant, but I was about to find out it was a much greater answer to the prayer than I could possibly ever imagined.

CHAPTER ELEVEN
"God Turns our World Upside-down"

The trip was all set. In July of 1986, we headed to Puerto Rico. The children were so excited to be able to go to the land where their dad was born. My older two boys barely remembered being in Puerto Rico when they were younger. The family there was excited they would finally meet the new grandchildren.

Lourdes' father, Dimas Rodgriguez, who was one of the founders of the Christian Charismatic Church, arranged for us to have services throughout the Island. This group had been formed by some men who had seen the Charismatic movement begin within the Catholic Church in Puerto Rico. The movement quickly spread, and a great revival of the Holy Spirit broke out. At first it had been embraced, but at one point, a new Bishop came and tried to put a lid on it. When these men found themselves confronted with either stopping their Holy Spirit retreats or leaving the Church, after prayer, they decided to leave the church rather than quench the Spirit of God. They formed churches throughout the Island, and in the Dominican Republic. Dimas was one of these men. In all, there were forty churches that were founded. I was excited to go with Charles Lewis to some of these churches and to hear him preach. He had been in Africa previously, and God used him greatly there. He was a great preacher of the Word, and God used him in healing. Sergio would translate, and I brought a few song tracks along to sing. I only had English songs, as I didn't know any in Spanish, and even though I had had those dreams, I only spoke a little conversational Spanish, and understood very little of what I heard others speak.

To my great surprise, when we arrived at these churches, many of them knew of me. I couldn't imagine how, but they would ask me, "Are you the sister of the prophecies?" I found out that Dimas had received the prophecies, and had felt such an anointing on them, that he felt moved by the Spirit of God to translate them into Spanish. He began to share them with people throughout the Island, which is how the people knew of me. It really surprised me, but then I remembered the vision of God blowing those papers throughout the earth. I marveled at what God was doing.

After going to several churches, one day Dimas told us about a wonderful evangelist from Puerto Rico who had crusades all over the world. Thousands upon thousands had been saved and healed through this man's ministry. Dimas asked us if we would like to go and see his ministry. Of course, we were very excited. (What Dimas didn't tell me was that he had taken the prophecies to this ministry as well.) His ministry was located on the other side of the Island, so we left early the next morning. The name of the ministry is Cristo Viene, which means Christ is Coming. It was a large three story building, which had many evangelists working there. The leader is evangelist Yiye Avila, a former body builder and teacher, who came to Christ and began sharing the gospel on street corners and parks. Thousands were saved and great miracles occurred when he prayed for the sick. He held crusades in all the Spanish speaking world. So many requests came in for crusades, that he began inviting other evangelists to join his team. The ministry had quickly become one of the largest in the Spanish world. Being from Louisiana, I had never heard of this man before, or seen him minister. Many said he was the Billy Graham of the Latin world, so I was very interested in visiting his ministry. When we arrived, we entered the building and headed past some offices and a publishing area towards a larger office. We stood outside, while Dimas entered to speak with someone. While we were standing there, I felt the presence of the Lord and began to pray. As I prayed I saw a vision of a short, well built, white haired man, who was praying. The Lord gave me a "message" to give this man. I opened my eyes and looked around, but I didn't see anyone who looked like this man. We went into an inner office, and to my surprise, the secretary seemed delighted to meet me. I thought these people were the friendliest people I had ever met. On one wall I saw a portrait of the man I had just seen in the vision. Underneath the portrait was the name "Yiye Avila". So now I knew who the message was for.

I mentioned to Dimas that God had just given me a vision of this man, and a message to give him. He conveyed this to the secretary, who seemed delighted, but she informed Dimas that Yiye had been in prayer and fasting for the last few days, and no one was allowed to go in to his office to speak with him at this time. Dimas explained this to me, and at that point, I asked him to ask if Yiye could read English. I was informed that he could, so I requested a paper and began to write down the message. At that point, the Lord spoke to my heart and said, "No, you are going to see him." I continued writing, discussing the issue with the Lord in my head. "But God, they just said no one can go in and see him", I told the Lord. "You are to see him", the Lord replied. "I can't just knock on his door and interrupt him", I responded to the Lord, but God was so insistent, that I finally said, "Lord, if this is really You, and You want me to see him, he's in there praying right now, can't You tell him to come out or something?" To my surprise, a few minutes later, a piece of paper appeared from under the shut door. The secretary picked it up and read, "Let the sister, and those that are with her, come in." It was amazing, as the secretary had not called him or sent a note to him about us being there, to my knowledge, so I knew it was God answering my prayer.

When we entered the office, the first thing I noticed was how humble an office it was. Then I met Yiye Avila. He was the warmest, most humblest man I had ever met. He seemed truly delighted to meet us. He stood there holding my hand in his, telling me how blessed he had been by my prophecies. I explained to him what God had shown me while I was praying, and he began to rejoice and thank the Lord. The message did not make a lot of sense to me, but it seemed to mean a lot to him. He said it was the answer to why he was praying and fasting. (I don't remember what the message to him was, but then, it wasn't a message for me, it was for him). He then said something in Spanish but I only understood two words, "radio" and "mañana". I knew he was saying something about being on the radio tomorrow. The Lord told me to tell him, "si", so I did. My husband was surprised, as he thought perhaps I had not fully understood the question. You see, Yiye had asked me to speak on his radio program the next day, and it was usually a thirty minute program, but he was going to extend it to an hour program. It would be heard throughout the Island and in the Dominican Republic! Now, I didn't get all that, but Sergio did, and he was surprised at my saying "si". I couldn't understand why God wanted me to do this radio program, when I wasn't a preacher in English, let alone in Spanish, and I had never spoken on a radio before. It was such a strange thing, but I had such a peace about it. I knew God was in control, and He didn't need me to understand in order to be obedient.

The next morning we started out bright and early to head back to the ministry. I was nervous, but God kept reassuring me. I didn't have a message in English, so how was I suppose to bring one in Spanish? I spent the ride with my eyes closed in prayer. At one point, I heard the sound of wings, and I saw this vision of all kinds of demonic creatures blocking the road ahead. These angels descended and fought with these demons and opened a pathway for us to go through. At that point, Dimas spoke and said something was wrong up ahead, and we needed to pray. The road was blocked off with policemen turning cars around. I told them the vision I had just had. As we inched forward in the traffic, every car was being told to make a u-turn and was not allowed to proceed. The only vehicles permitted to pass were emergency vehicles. We were in a yellow Datsun station wagon, but when it was our turn in front of the traffic police, they motioned for us to go through. Dimas sat there stunned for a moment, but Sergio told him, "Step on it, brother". When I looked back, I saw them turn the car behind us around, and the other car after that. There was no obvious reason as to why we were allowed to go through and no one else was, other than the Lord. Everyone in the car knew that something supernatural was happening, and we were certain God wanted us to go to that program. (We found out later that there had been an explosion in one of the pharmaceutical plants on that road. It was a major explosion and many were injured and eight people had died. The only cars being allowed through were emergency vehicles only. The only thing I can surmise is the police officers must have seen us as an emergency vehicle.)

Even with the delay, we arrived a few minutes early. To my surprise, no one was working in the ministry. They were all upstairs in the ministry room on the third floor, where they broadcasted their radio programs from. They were waiting to hear me preach! I got very nervous at this point and went out on the terrace to pray. I was shaking, as all these people were waiting to hear ME speak, and I didn't have anything to say! What had God gotten me in to? I stood there trembling wondering why in the world God would ask me to speak to these people, when He spoke to my heart and said, "This is a divine appointment. For this reason you were born. I will use you to speak to many people; fear not. It is not you who will speak, it is I who will speak through you." I had a choice, to believe it was God speaking, or that I had gone crazy. I decided it was more important to obey God. If I was delusional, I would embarrass myself, but I wasn't concerned about what everyone thought of me, I just wanted to please God.

Right before the program was to start, I asked Sergio, "How do Christian's greet each other in Spanish?" He told me, "Dios te bendiga", which means, "God bless you." I knew how to say my name and where I was from in Spanish, so I figured I start out with that, and trust God to take over. I had those dreams, but I hadn't understood them. I might have been preaching in Spanish in my sleep, but I had no idea of what to do while I was awake. One thing I did know was faith. I knew God was able to do anything, including giving me the ability to speak in Spanish at a moments notice. I had this sense of His presence all over me. Looking back, I can't explain how I stepped up to do such a thing. It had to be the Spirit of God leading me.

When I was called to the microphone, I started out saying, "Dios te bendiga; mi nombre es Charlene Ramirez. Soy una ama de casa de Louisiana..." (God bless you; my name is Charlene Ramirez; I'm a housewife from Louisiana). Then suddenly, God took over. For the next forty-five minutes, God spoke in fluent Spanish through my mouth! The people most surprised about this were myself and my husband. We were the only two who knew for real that I DIDN"T SPEAK SPANISH! I knew a few words, but this was unbelievable. Sergio knew it was the Lord speaking through me. I had no idea what I was saying, but I did catch a word or two that I understood. I saw some of these evangelists fall to their knees in tears. At one point I thought to myself, "Either this is God saying something amazing, or they are on their knees praying God will shut up my babbling". It was the most amazing experience I have ever had.

When God finished speaking, people came up to me for prayer. Sergio was next to me. They would speak to me, as if they thought I understood, but I didn't. How was I to explain to them the woman they had just heard preaching in fluent Spanish, didn't understand anything they were saying? I surmised they wanted prayer, so Sergio and I prayed for them. To my amazement, God spoke to many of them in Spanish, giving them personal prophetic messages (Sergio told me later). I have no idea what I said to them, but they seemed extremely touched and blessed. The call center had phone calls coming in from all over. For four hours people kept calling in! People had been saved and had been blessed by the message the Lord had brought to them through me. On the way home, Sergio told me what the Lord had said through my mouth. God had blessed the Island and encouraged His people. He was totally amazed at what the Lord had done. I was in awe, and exhausted.

We received so many calls to minister throughout Puerto Rico but our return flight was already set for the following Monday. We were asked to speak on another radio program at a local church, which we were able to make, as it was the day before our flight. Again, the Lord moved, and I preached in Spanish, as I had before. It seemed obvious the Lord had begun something special. It wasn't just a one time occurrence. Now, we knew God was doing something in our lives, and we had some decisions to make.

I don't think either of us had any idea of what had happened. It was like something out of the book of Acts. I had only heard of a couple missionaries who had said they experienced God's intervention while out in the mission field, enabling them to speak in the language of the people in front of them. I didn't know any of them personally, I had just heard a testimony once over the radio, and read about it in a Christian publication. They were missionaries or ministers, but me, who was I? After the months of poverty and struggles, how could this all be happening to me? Sometimes it felt as if I was dreaming. I wasn't some great preacher, or a giant of faith. I didn't have any experience, no degree of any kind, so perhaps it was just a once in a lifetime event. God must have used me in that moment because He had something to say, and no one available to speak it. But there were so many ministers around, my husband and Charles, the evangelist we were accompanying there, so why didn't God use them to speak? It was all so overwhelming. The dreams had me preaching in Spanish, and now it had come true. Could it be God was calling me to be a preacher, a messenger of His word? Why would He choose me? Didn't He know how weak and insecure I was? I had been obedient to do what He wanted, when He wanted, and I guessed that was my answer, I was obedient. I remember reading in the Bible how God used a donkey to talk, so I guessed He could speak through whoever He wanted to.

The key was surrendering and being obedient, as well as believing God can do the impossible. Simple faith was all I had, and that was all He needed.

CHAPTER TWELVE
"A ministry is born"

When we returned to Louisiana, we knew our life was changed. Here we were back home, where everything was the same, no job, no money, but we were totally changed. We had no doors open in Louisiana, but dozens of open doors to minister in Puerto Rico. We knew God was calling us to follow Him. We shared the wonderful story of what had happened with our church and all our friends. They too were totally amazed. We decided to sell everything we had and return to Puerto Rico, as the Lord was leading.

It was hard to say good-bye to everyone. The church had a farewell service for us. People blessed us and the money was raised to pay for us to return. They prayed over us, and sent us off with so much love. The children were excited about going to live in a rainforest. It was like living on vacation to them, but there would be complications, as none of them spoke Spanish. We would have to home school them until they could learn. It was hard for them to decide what toys they could keep. We would be allowed three suitcases per person, for a total of eighteen bags. How do you pack everything for a family of six in eighteen bags? We had to take all of their school books with us, and then there was our personal important documents, and photo albums. We managed to eliminate almost everything in the hopes that we would replace it somehow once we were over there. The children kept their favorite toys, whatever fit into a backpack for each of them. It was difficult, but exciting. Sergio's parents owned a house in the country, in the middle of the rainforest. They had a small cottage on the property that had belonged to an uncle. We would be able to stay there and borrow their old car, but past that, we had no idea what was ahead. It was indeed a venture of faith!

We had two cars, one that Deidra had given us, and another which was given to us by another family at church. We gave one car to a brother from church who's car had blown the engine. He was unemployed as well, and had a job offer, but he had to have a car in order to take the job. He cried and hugged Sergio when he gave him the car. The other car we drove to Florida, with everything packed on top. We gave it to my sister and flew to Puerto Rico. We had left all our earthly possessions, except for personal items and clothing, whatever we could carry with us, and had launched ourselves, by faith, into the mission field where the Lord was calling us.

My father-in-law picked us up at the airport and took us home. We stayed in their house at first, while we tried to fix up the cottage. We had a couple of beds that family gave us, but not much else. We had a small electric burner to cook on, and a old refrigerator. Eventually, a Christian gave us a sofa and table. It was humble, but it was home. We had to wash our clothes by hand and hang them out; we didn't even have hot water at first, so we bathed in the cold water, when there was water. The electricity and water went out frequently. The hardships were many, but we were together, and the peace of God filled our hearts.

Dimas got to work and called many churches. Before long, we had services throughout the Island.
Sometimes we would preach almost every night. The Lord continued to move, ministering to the people in Spanish. God did marvelous things. People were saved; people were healed. We had no sponsors, or consistent support, and we didn't ask for money. The

churches always took up an offering, even though we did not ask, and it was always enough to meet our needs. We used my in-laws car to get around, until it broke down, then my brother-in-laws old car, until it broke down. A pastor gave us a little station wagon which ran fairly well, but the back doors would fly open if you leaned against them, so we had to be very careful of the children riding in it. Things weren't easy, but a missionary's life never is.

On one occasion we went to preach at a church where they were having communion before the message. The rule of this particular church was that only people who had been baptized in water were allowed to participate in communion. The two oldest boys had been baptized at First Assembly, but Sharon and David had not been baptized yet. Sharon had given her life to Jesus when she was very small, but she understood what it meant. She loved the Lord and wanted to participate in communion. We had often had communion at home together, plus at church in Lafayette, as a family. She understood that was what you did as a Christian to remember the Lord Jesus. I tried to quietly explain to her that this church had a rule that only those who had been baptized could take communion. She began to cry, so I took her outside and tried to explain that it was their rule, not God's or ours, but she kept saying, "but I want to remember the Lord too." Clearly, she didn't understand. The rest of the week she kept asking us when she could be baptized. She said she didn't want to not be able to "remember the Lord in communion ever again." This had obviously upset her more than I realized. We decided to take the children down to the river and baptize her. Of course, David wanted to be baptized too. So Sergio and I went with all the children and had a service at the river and baptized them.

When Sharon came out of the water, she sat down on a rock and then started to cry. I asked her what was the matter, and she said she was sad because she couldn't speak in tongues too. I tried to explain to her, but I could see she was very determined. She wanted ALL of Jesus! I still remember her saying, "But mommy, I don't know how to speak in tongues yet!" I told her that it wasn't about knowing how to, it was just something that God gives people and perhaps it would happen to her when she was older, after all, she was only four years old. That didn't seem to quench her thirst! When we returned home, she went into the bathroom and locked the door. She was in there for a long time. When she came out she had a big smile on her face. I asked her what had happened and she told me she locked herself in there to talk to God about this being filled with the Spirit and speaking in tongues, and she didn't want to come out until He gave it to her too. Well, God honored her faith, and she said she received it, so she decided she could come out of the bathroom now! What a precious story! How God honors childlike faith!

Let me explain this, Puerto Rico has a large Pentecostal population. There are churches practically on every street corner. The fact that we were independent opened doors for us to visit many different types of churches. There was a heavy Pentecostal influence over the church, and some of the churches were very strict in observing laws and regulations. Christian women didn't use pants, makeup or jewelry. I had to adapt in order not to offend anyone. Some churches were more open, but others were extremely legalistic. In order to bring the word God had given to me, I became, as Paul said, a Greek to the Greeks, a Roman to the Romans.

People began to ask if we had audio cassettes of our preachings. We handed out as many typed messages as we could, but we realized there were too many messages, and too many people. Dimas started investigating how we could publish these messages into a book. We took some of the audio messages that had been taped in various services and duplicated them. We sold them for a little more than cost, to help offset some of the ministry expenses. These cassettes started going everywhere. We preached several radio programs as well, and before long, the ministry was well known.

As God had promised before, when He gave me the vision of the messages landing all over the world, one day a letter came from somewhere in France, then Spain, then Cuba, Venezuela, and finally from as far away as South Africa. I was amazed that the prophecies had reached places where I had never sent them! How they got there, only God knows! The letter from South Africa said they had taken some of them and translated them into Zulu and taken them to some tribes! I was astounded. Everything God had shown me when we were back in Louisiana going through all those struggles, was now coming to pass.

Letters came from the United States as well. In June of 1987, A pastor from New Jersey invited us to come and preach at his inauguration service for his new church. We prayed about it, and God told us to go, telling us we would be there for almost a "season". We didn't have the money for the flight, but God spoke to Sergio that He would provide. The Lord also told Sergio He would provide us a car while we were there for four-hundred dollars. When we told some people this, they laughed and said you couldn't get a bicycle for that in the New York area. Still, God sent a brother to our door who told us the Lord had spoken to him to give us four hundred dollars. We had not told him what the Lord had told us, but he said God had spoken to him while he was in prayer, and told him to give us four hundred dollars. We took it as a sign from the Lord; it was the confirmation of our trip. God provided just enough for us to buy one-way tickets for the six of us to Newark, New Jersey. We only had one service scheduled, and had no idea where we would stay. With our tickets, the four-hundred dollars (for the car) and our children, we flew to New Jersey. A deacon from the church came to pick us up at the airport. He and his wife had no children, and they had a basement studio apartment that we were welcome to stay in for as long as the Lord had us there. Praise God, we had a place to stay!

The pastor of the church called us once we settled in and asked if we would be willing to go with him to his radio program and minister in two days. Of course, we were honored to, and we had a feeling God was going to do another miraculous thing. We went the next day with the dear people who had taken our family in, Eduardo and Maria Escobar, to site see in New York City. They were such sweet Christians. They opened their home, cooked for us, took us around. They treated us like long-lost family. They loved my children, and my children loved them! We took our first subway ride, which was a pretty scary experience. All the while we were in New York City, I kept feeling the presence of the Lord. I felt this overwhelming feeling of judgment over the city.

When we returned home that evening, we spent some time in prayer with Eduardo and Maria. The Lord gave me a vision of the city while we were in prayer. I saw the city, by night, with this glow from lights coming from the southern part of the city. I could see a news helicopter hovering over the area, and I heard them reporting that the destruction was devastating. Then, it was as if I was on the ground, and it was daylight. It was hard to see, as there was this dust all in the air. I could see through the dust, some workers with masks on. They were searching through rubble. The rubble was piled high. I heard one say that they didn't think they would find any more people alive. It seemed as if the city had been shaken by something that brought a few buildings to rubble. At the time, I supposed it to be an earthquake. I went on the radio the next day and shared the vision with the people. God began to speak to the city through that program. God called the church to pray for the city. The Spirit of the Lord began to speak as He had that day in Puerto Rico; when the message ended, I looked and saw the leaders of the radio station standing and listening, visually touched. The program had gone over the time limit, but they did not cut it, they extended it in order to hear all the Lord was saying. Once again, the phones rang. All the lines lit up. Sergio, Dimas, and I were taking service requests and praying for people over the phone for two hours. When it was all over, we had services lined up all over New Jersey, New York, and even in Connecticut. We began preaching all over the New York area as a result.

The radio station asked us to come back again. In one of the programs, a lady called in for prayer for her daughter who was a diabetic. The child was only three years old and had to be injected four times a day. She cried as she told us that her child would cry and run from her every time she would go near her for fear of another injection. It broke this poor mother's heart, and mine as well. She was a Catholic woman, but had been listening to the radio and heard the message. She wondered if we could pray for her child to be healed. I prayed with her over the phone. Then she asked where we would be preaching, because she wanted to meet us. She came that night with her child and her husband. She came to the altar at the end of the service and gave her life to the Lord. She brought her daughter for us to meet her and we prayed for the child. The next night she came back with her sister and her niece, and they gave their life to the Lord. She went to several more services we held in the area, and continued to bring family members, and God kept saving her family. The amazing thing was that when she took her child for a check up, they said the child's sugar level was normal. They reduced her to only one shot a day, just in case, they said, but they couldn't explain what had happened. The whole family came to Christ because of this miracle! (The last I heard from this family was that they eventually returned to the Dominican Republic and started a home church there).

In one of our radio programs, a church leader called us from a church in Elizabeth, New Jersey. We were invited to go and minister in his church. When we arrived there, we met with the pastor as well as the elders of the church. I had a feeling this church would be different, and I wasn't mistaken. When the service started, to my delight, the congregation began to worship God with hands lifted, and before long, almost everyone was dancing! This church had over 200 people! It was an amazing thing to see all these people dancing and praising God with such enthusiasm. They praised the Lord like this for almost 2 hours! It was if no one wanted to stop. It was nearly 10pm when they called me to the microphone to preach the message!

I was concerned about it being so late, thinking perhaps I should be brief, but they told me that they rarely got out of church before midnight, and to give them all the Lord had for them. What hunger and dedication! The Spirit of God moved mightily there because they were putting Him first.

The Lord spoke to His people that night, and lives that were there for the first time flooded the altars. People were saved, people were healed; it was totally amazing! We had taken some cassettes with us, and my children set up a table outside the church to set them on when the service was over. It was crazy! People flooded the table and bought everything within minutes. The pastor went to Sergio and asked how many tapes we had brought with us. Sergio told him probably about 50. He laughed at him and told him, "You can't come here with only that!" Then he invited us to come back the next Saturday night, and told us to bring several hundred tapes with us. We could not believe it! We spent the rest of the week making copies, in between the other services we had, and returned the following Saturday night, and preached again. What loving people were there. We had never enjoyed preaching a service as much as we did there. People were so open to the Word of God. It was the most joyous place I had ever visited. God moved again, as He had the first time. Since they were in no hurry, the Lord had total freedom to speak, and He did! There were many prophetic words spoken to the church and to individuals, and it was well after midnight by the time we were done. All the tapes sold again. It was such a memorable time. It felt like we had gone back in time and were part of the first church. We left there so blessed, spiritually as well as financially.

After we had been in the New York area for two months preaching, the Lord gave me a word for Chicago. How in the world were we going to get to Chicago? As of yet, the four hundred dollar car had not appeared. We hadn't needed it yet. Eduardo would take us to services, and Dimas was there, with a car from a family relative who lived in the area, but how were we suppose to get all the way to Chicago?

Now we knew why God had spoken to us back in Puerto Rico about the car! Then a call came in from a church in Chicago, asking us to go preach there. It seems someone from their church had been in New York and had seen us minister in a service there, and returned with the information to their church in Chicago. The Lord had already spoken to me that we were to go there, so I said yes, by faith. We continued to pray, and to look in ads for a used car, but to no avail. We mentioned over the radio in another program, that we were interested in buying a good used car. We didn't say the amount we had. A Christian called us to say he was working on a car for a pastor friend of his, and the pastor wanted to sell it. When we asked how much, he told us four hundred dollars. We immediately told him we'd take it. We went to meet the pastor and he invited us to preach in his church. We bought the car from him. Since we were going to take the trip to Chicago, he put all new tires and had a tune up done on it for us, in other words, he put what we paid for it back into the car to get it road ready for us. Now we had a car! God had done exactly what He said He would do!

Dimas informed us there was a Charismatic church from the group which formed in Puerto Rico that was located in Lancaster, Pennsylvania. He made a call to the pastor and let him know we would be traveling through, and the pastor invited us to preach in Lancaster. It was a small church, but we loved the people and the area. We stayed for several days at the pastor's home, and then continued on from there to Chicago. The church we ministered in was a small church, but they also had a radio program, so we were able to minister by radio to the Spanish Christian population in Chicago as well. God spoke to the city, and a week after we left, the great storm the Lord spoke of, hit the Chicago area. By then we were on our way to Florida. We ministered in a few churches in Florida, visited my parents, and then flew back to Puerto Rico. In all, we were gone for just shy of three months, "a season".

102

Visiting my parents before going to Puerto Rico
(left to right) Charlene, Christian, Chad, mother, Sharon,
Dad, and David

CHAPTER THIRTEEN
"Back home in the Caribbean"

We arrived back home to our little house in the rain forest with great testimonies to share of all the things the Lord had done, but we didn't get much time to rest. Days were spent with working with the children in home school, washing clothes by hand, cooking for us and for my in-laws, (which often included my nieces), and of course, spending time with God. He continued to give me messages which I would type up, give to brother Dimas, and he would translate them and make copies. Many people wanted to receive these words from the Lord, so we mailed out to quite a lot of people who had signed up to be on our newsletter list. Then there were services throughout the island. Sometimes we would have crusades and stay over night with a pastor or member of the congregation, which meant having people coming by for prayer all day long. It was a very busy time, but very rewarding at the same time. We made some Christian friends that were involved with prison outreach, and before long, we were visiting the prisons as well. Someone from a Christian rehab ministry approached us, having heard Sergio's testimony, and asked if we would be interested in coming and sharing at some of their rehab homes. We were delighted to go, and in particular, Sergio really felt led to involve himself in talking to these men. As a former addict to alcohol, he could really relate to them, and so he went almost weekly to minister to them.

We had made great friends with several of the evangelists at Yiye Avila's ministry as well. We would always stop in at the ministry whenever we were on that side of the island. We went to many of the Crusades that Yiye had, when he was in Puerto Rico. His ministry was an amazing ministry. Thousands would come to Christ, and I saw some great miracles occur whenever he prayed for the sick. He was such a dynamic preacher, yet such a simple, humble man. The people just loved him, and he loved them. I was so thankful to get to know this man and his ministry; he made a profound impact on me and on our ministry. I had never seen such dedication and humbleness in any of the large ministries in the States. This man had a humble home, the same one he had for years, and when his car wore out, he didn't even buy a new one. He said he had plenty of people who could pick him up. He spent every dime on reaching out to souls. Finally, all the pastors in the island got together and bought him a car and a new suit. (He always wore the same old suits, as he didn't have the time to waste on shopping for clothes, neither was it of any importance to him). That's just the way he was, totally focused, totally dedicated to bringing lives to Christ. Perhaps that's why God used him so mightily. The last thing he would want is for me to go on and on about him, "it's all about Jesus", he often said.

One day Yiye invited me to come to a retreat at the ministry. We were honored to be asked to go. When we arrived, it was a great surprise to us that Yiye was reading to his staff some of the prophecies God had given me. He asked me to comment on them. He told me how the Lord had showed him many things, and how he had been led to pray concerning many of them. It had blessed him, and he wanted to share it with all of his staff. I was so humbled by this man. I know it was the Lord who had written them, I was just a "secretary" taking dictation, but it still brings me to tears to realize the Lord could have used someone like me to be a blessing to others. I remembered how I had cried out to God that He was wasting His time using me, but seeing this servant of God so blessed by these writings, made me realize why God always uses the weak and foolish things of this world to confound the wise. I am humbled that He chose me to be one of His messengers. Thank you Lord!

Another wonderful thing happened, we were able to publish some of the first prophecies into a book. It was costly, but the Lord provided. Dimas was the moving force behind it. He contacted a publishing house in the Dominican Republic, and made arrangements. Several book stores carried them, and our dear friend Yiye Avila carried them in his ministry. He printed some of the prophecies in his news magazine, which went worldwide, and before long we started receiving letters from around the globe.

On one occasion, there was a prayer night at Yiye's ministry, and we were invited. When we got there, the prayer was already in session. People were kneeling and praying all over the building. We entered in quietly and knelt in prayer in a corner. While I was praying, the Lord showed me a vision: I saw the island of Puerto Rico as if I was up in the upper atmosphere. I saw this tower go up from the Island. It let off this light that went up into space, and from there, it split and came back down, bringing light to places all over the earth. I went to Yiye to tell him what the Lord had shown me. He began to leap for joy. Unknown to me, he had called the prayer meeting because he was seeking confirmation as to whether he should buy a local television station and go into a television ministry. Since he knew I didn't know this, he took it as confirmation from the Lord, and bought the station. It was a small station with only a local area outreach. He launched the television ministry, and we were asked to join one of the evangelists on one of the programs. We had an hour program called "Encuentro de Amistad", which means "An Encounter with Friends". It was a talk show, where we discussed the things the Lord was revealing, interviewed guests, and prayed for our viewers. The television ministry grew rapidly. Before long, they purchased another station, then another. It was known as "La Cadena de Milagro" (The Miracle Chain). Our program was being seen throughout the Island,

and it brought us more preaching engagements around the island. We preached several crusades, an open air crusade in a soccer field, a crusade in a town square, and a youth convention in an sports arena. God moved mightily in these services.

At the same time the Lord was moving mightily through Sergio as well. When our ministry first started, there were those who thought it wasn't right that the woman was the one ministering. Sergio had put his ministry aside in order to support God's leading in my life. It takes quite a man to recognize God's moving in the life of his wife, and be willing to support her. But God had a plan for Sergio in the ministry as well. Those first few months it seemed as if all he did was drive me back and forth. I remember him telling those who questioned him about it, "If God calls me to be her chauffeur, then that's what I'll be. This is God's ministry and His doing, not mine." How proud I was to be with a man who was so humbly submitted to the Lord. But one afternoon in prayer, God told me the time had come. He instructed me to bring the message to the church, but instead of ministering after, I was to call Sergio. God was going to use him to minister and pray for the people. I told Sergio, and he asked if I was sure, and I told him "yes". That night I called him when I was done preaching, (which is rather unusual, as usually the person preaching gives the altar call and ministers). Sergio had been in prayer throughout the message. He took the microphone and God began to move! God began to speak to individuals through him. He called lives to the altar, and the altar was filled. He prayed for them and for the sick, and the Lord began healing people. It was truly amazing! And just like in the dream the Lord had given me years before, there were a lot of people, and he asked me to help him pray for them all. The dream had come to pass!

Over the next few months, the Lord continued to use him, especially in personal prophecy, but in healing as well. He was not only involved in the prison and rehab ministry, but began preaching in churches which invited him. Sometimes we had simultaneous services, with me in one church, and him in another. It wasn't always easy, balancing the ministry and our family life. We took the children with us as much as possible. The older ones would help with the sales of the cassettes and books. If the trip was too long, often my in-laws would keep the children. The children seemed happy having a rain forest to play in. Grandpa had chickens, geese, dogs and cats for them to play with, and they found it fun living in a virtual "jungle". They were still being home schooled, and doing very well, but they had little interaction with other children, other than their step brother and sister and their cousins. Sharon and David were still very young, and having all the animals and the wildlife was a great adventure. But for Christian and Chad, especially Chad, the lack of friends their age was becoming a problem, one that I wasn't as aware of as I should have been. We did get to spend a lot of "down" time together, taking the children to the beach or on hikes, and then there were crusades in other parts of the island where we spent time site-seeing in between the evening services with them.

We returned to preach in the New York area again, and this time doors opened to go and preach in Boston and Providence, as well as in Washington DC. The children enjoyed going to see so many things that they had only read about. We had the opportunity to reunite with my sisters, Elaine and Barbara, and their families in Pennsylvania. I had not seen them in almost twenty years, (although we did keep up with what was going on in our lives through my dad). We used to go and visit them when I was little, but they were from my father's first marriage and were teenagers when I was born. My memories of them were childhood memories. I was at my oldest sister Elaine's wedding, and then they came to my sister Gail's wedding when I was fourteen. My oldest niece was only seven years younger than I was. It was a great reunion. We finally reconnected on an adult level and all of our children got to know their distant cousins. They seemed extremely interested and surprised about the fact that I had become a minister and had so many questions about it all. It was an wonderful experience being able to share what the Lord had done in my life with all of them.

We also stayed several weeks in a beach house when we visited my parents, and got to take the children to Disney World. My parents had moved from the east coast of Florida to the west coast after my father had a stroke. He was left with one arm being paralyzed, but we had prayed, and God had restored the use of his arm completely. I loved the times we had together. We didn't see each other a lot, but it was quality time. I called them frequently, and wrote letters, but we only saw each other about once a year. My parents were always very supportive of me. They were glad I had found my true love and I was happy. I think they wished I had a little more stable life, but they recognized I had a passion for the things of God and the missionary life serving God made me happy. True, we never knew where our next dime was coming from, and we had nothing as far as worldly goods, but we had God and we had each other. The children had an unusual life, but it was filled with adventures. I always felt as long as we were all together, and doing God's will, it was the best for us all. I recognize that my children had to make some sacrifices, but God blessed them with so many special things, things that most children only dream about.

I realize now, in looking back, that this lifestyle affected some of the children in positive ways, and others in negative ways. There are always consequences in life for the choices we make, and it is true that you can't please everyone, or always do what's best for everyone. The best anyone can do is serve the Lord, and trust Him to resolve any issues that might arise. I say these things, because in April of 1979, my oldest child, Chad, left and went to live with his father. He left me a note saying he didn't want to live a missionary life anymore, he wanted a settled, normal life. It was one of the hardest moments in my life. I had told the Lord I would serve Him, follow Him, no matter what. Now the hardest thing I had to face, the one thing I prayed would never happen, happened. I was devastated, and so were the children. My son was on a plane halfway to Minnesota when I came home and found the note. We managed to get the airline to put him on a phone when the plane landed, and he cried and begged me to let him have a chance to live with his dad and try having a "normal" life. At that moment, it made me realize the cost my ministry was having on my children. I felt the Lord with me, and He helped me make the toughest decision any mother ever has to make, to let go.

I can't begin to explain the next few days and weeks that followed. The sadness I felt was like a deep pit that sucked me in. It was as if someone had died. I would try to do regular things, but this depression was overwhelming. Just going to the grocery store and seeing his favorite cereal made me leave in tears and rush home. I felt like such a failure as a mother. How could I have not seen how my choices were affecting him? What about the other children? I decided to fast and pray until God would tell me why this happened and what I was to do now. On the evening of the second day of fasting, the Lord spoke to me. He let me know that this was not something He had done, or that the devil had done. This was an issue of my son's free will; it was his choice. He revealed to me that my priorities and my son's priorities were not the same, but if I was willing to let go and trust God, the Lord would take care of him and help him to find his way. God promised me that He would return my son back to me one day, if I would just trust Him. Then He told me to stop fasting because I was pregnant! I took a home pregnancy test, and indeed I was pregnant. It seemed like the worst time for another child, but God knew my heart, and how I was doubting my ability as a mother. The fact the Lord was sending me another child, was His way of letting me know that I wasn't a failure as a mother. He was entrusting me with another life. I can't say it was always easy after that, or that the tears were all wiped away, but the horrible depression left me. Sergio and the children were delighted about the news, and it helped us heal from the hurt of loosing Chad. (A child can never replace another child, but new life always brings new hope.)

I kept in touch with my son through letters and phone calls. It was such a time of adjustment for us all. He seemed happy being in a high school, in a normal life. He got involved in sports, and was a straight A student. While I was happy that he was doing well and was so happy, I missed him terribly. I tried to keep busy so that I wouldn't allow myself to sink back into the depression, but it wasn't easy. The children missed him as well, especially Christian. Chad was his playmate, all of his life. Chris was a shy boy, and Chad was outgoing, but now Chris had to step up and be the "big brother". While it was hard for him, he has told me that in many ways, it was the making of him. He felt he was always a tag along, following in his big brother's shadow; then he was thrust into the position of being the oldest, being the one responsible, and while it was hard, it helped him develop leadership abilities which he has used throughout his life. While Chad leaving was a tragedy for me, for all of us, I am certain God had a purpose in letting it be so, for Chad's sake as well as ours. For one thing, it helped me to understand how heartbroken the Lord is when His children leave Him, something that one can only understand by experiencing it. And Chad excelled in school and developed a close relationship with his father, which he never had before. God tells us, "All things work together for good, to them that love the Lord, and are called, according to His purpose." Even the heartbreaks, the hardships, and the negative events in our life God can bring something good out of them.

Our home in the rain forest in Puerto Rico

CHAPTER FOURTEEN
"New Horizons"

We continued ministering throughout the island, and I had received several messages of warning for the Island. Although the churches had grown all over the island, the legalism had grown as well. For an island that is one hundred miles long by thirty five miles wide, there was sixteen Christian radio stations, four Christian television stations, and churches on almost every block. Now that sounds wonderful, but the reality of it was there were such divisions, that it had almost become a holy war. Some of the stations, that backed one group, would use air time to attack the other groups. It became ridiculous. Our brother, Yiye Avila, was one who didn't participate in such things. He tried desperately to bring peace between the different groups, only to often be attacked for doing so. The Lord sent me a message warning that this judgmental legalism had to stop. There was no love between these groups, and God was warning them to repent. I had a vision of great winds that came and blew away even the small, unripened fruits from the trees. The damage it caused was extensive. The Lord told the people if they did not repent and humble their pride, this storm would come. I was able to bring this warning over the radio and television. Sadly, many of the ministries continued with their attacks against the others. It got so bad that they were calling a Christian lady pastor a Jezebel because she cut her hair, and wore make-up and jewelry. They said women who wore pants were in sin and in danger of hell. It caused so much division and confusion. The self righteousness of these people was unbelievable. The danger of all this was that salvation by works was becoming the prevalent doctrine. I went on the radio and explained that true holiness comes from a relationship with Jesus Christ, and what He has done for us; we were made righteous, holy, by grace and faith in Jesus and it had nothing to do with what you wear. I was accused of not being a believer in "holiness", and many doors shut because of it.

At that time, the Lord began to speak more messages specifically for America. God told me I was to return to preach in the States, and that I would be preaching in Texas and California, which surprised me. We had never been out west before. Within two weeks of receiving this word from the Lord, I received two letters, one from a pastor in Texas, and another from a deacon of a church in Los Angeles. Both letters were invitations to come and preach at their churches. Having received the word from the Lord, Sergio and I took it as confirmation from the Lord, and began to look into airfare for us to go. We had left the $400 dollar car we had bought in New York, at my cousins house in Florida when we flew back to Puerto Rico. So we decided that all we needed was the airfare to Miami (which was much cheaper), and then we could drive out to California. Before long, God provided the money for our airfare, and we packed and left on this new ministry adventure in June of 1989.

We arrived in Miami, spent a few days with family, preached in a couple of churches in Florida, where we received the funds needed to embark on our journey, so we headed west. We stopped and preached in Louisiana and spent some time there with old friends. I was delighted to be invited to preach at the church we attended when we lived there. It was a wonderful experience preaching "at home". I have to admit I was very nervous at first. I had preached in so many places, and yet preaching a midweek service at Pastor King's church was very intimidating to me. The service went very well, and people were very touched. Pastor King invited us out to eat after the service and told me he was very proud of me. It was like having my father tell me. I can't tell you how important it was to have his approval. I looked up to him so much, and his "seal of approval" was a great blessing to me. We had a great time with all our dear friends in Lafayette. We shared all the wonderful testimonies we had seen in the ministry. We prayed for many of them. God had given us a special group of friends in Lafayette. Many of them had ministerial calls in their lives; some had prophetic calls. Our experiences were a great encouragement to them. When the week was up, it was difficult to leave them once again.

It wasn't easy traveling with three children while being pregnant. My stomach was quite large already. It turns out that when God had told me I was pregnant, I was already 4 months pregnant. Now I was almost 7 months pregnant. We stopped and preached at the church in Texas that had written us. It was a small church in Houston, Texas. It was a blessing, but I really wasn't sure why God had sent us there. Still, it was on the road to California. Each church we preached at gave us an offering which helped us cover the expenses of our trip and enabled us to continue forward. We made the long trip across the state of Texas. There were miles and miles of nothing. It was hard on the kids, but we played lots of games, and did some of our home school work. Still, it was an adventure, as we had never seen a desert before.

On the second day, a sand storm blew up as we were approaching El Paso, Texas. We could barely see where we were going, so we decided to stop and stay at a hotel there. The sand hit your legs and face as you tried to walk. It was awful. I remember saying, "Thank God we are just passing through and don't live in this place!" The children didn't like it either. (I learned later, never to say something like that.) The sand storm passed, and we were back on the road the next day. Desert stretched out before us for the next two days, as we crossed New Mexico and Arizona.

The desert has a majestic beauty, and you can see for miles and miles. We made a stop at a real "ghost town". I made sandwiches in the car for the kids, and they hopped out to explore with sandwich in hand, only to come a few minutes later to ask why I had given them such hard bread. In the matter of a few minutes, the dryness evaporated every drop of moisture from the bread, leaving it as hard as a crouton! Yes, it was a different world out there! It has such a majestic, strange beauty. I did a lot of praying while we were in the desert. I understand why God called his servants to this "wilderness", to commune with them, including his son Jesus. It is a place of solitude and stillness, where you can focus on the Lord.

We arrived in Los Angeles, California, with great joy. It was a trip I had always wanted to make, and the kids were excited to see the Pacific Ocean, and all the sites like Hollywood, Beverly Hills, and Disneyland! We were invited to stay at the deacon's house, who had written us. That was an experience! They had a small home that already had 8 people living there. Still, they gave us the master bedroom, and we made up sleeping bags on the floor for our children. We had spent all the money we had on the trip to get out there, so we were thankful for being housed, even if it was tight quarters. There was only one bathroom, so we pretty much had to "take a number". Still, they were a loving family that generously opened their door to us, and were very excited to have us there. We had a crusade at their church that week. It was awesome. The place was full, and different churches visited on different nights. God moved, speaking to the people and the city of Los Angeles. We were invited to preach in several other churches while we were there. We were very blessed when we left 3 weeks later.

We headed to take the children to see the Grand Canyon, which was an amazing site. Little Sharon was more interested in feeding the wildlife there, then observing the great canyon before us. We then traveled through the Painted Desert, and north into Colorado to see the Rocky Mountains, on our way to Chicago and then New York. When we arrived in Colorado, the children noticed the snow on the very tops of the Rockies. They had never seen snow. They wanted to go way up there to see the snow, but we let them know you can't go up to the peak of the mountains. Still, they were insistent that they wanted to "touch" the snow. They remembered that we had always told them that if they would get together and pray, God would answer them. Well, they got together and prayed in the back seat of the car, for God to make it snow! We were up in the mountains, near Vail, Colorado, but the temperature was in the 60's. We stopped at a hotel for the night. Sergio and I did not want to discourage their faith, but it was mid-summer! In the morning, the children jumped out of bed to look out the window, hoping to see snow, but the ground was green and flowers were blooming everywhere. They were disappointed, but we tried to reassure them by agreeing to take a mountain route that would at least bring them a little closer to view the mountain tops. As we traveled up the road, the sun was shining, and the temperature was in the low 60's. Soon it clouded over, and it became colder. To our surprise, the temperature dropped 30 degrees, and snow flurries began! We pulled over and let the children out to play in the "snow". They jumped up and down, praising the Lord for sending them snow! God sure is good! A bus load of tourists stopped and got out to take pictures of this "rare" sight, snow falling at the end of June! Snow stayed on the slopes, and the children were able to play in it. Ah, the faith of a child! We can learn so much from them. They have never forgotten this experience.

We stopped in Minnesota to see Chad. It was a hard time for us all. It was a bittersweet reunion, for all of us. It was great to see him, but very hard to leave again. He was doing well in school, and happy in his new life, but we all missed each other. Still, we couldn't stay long because we couldn't afford to stay in hotels much longer. I cried most of the way to Chicago. We visited the church we had gone to previously, and were able to minister in a few others. God continued to call people to repentance, and our nation to return to God. The amazing thing we found as we traveled around the country preaching in Hispanic congregations, was the amount of Hispanics who have come to Christ after coming to the United States. Across the board, about 80 percent of every church we have been in, came to know Jesus after they immigrated to America. It has been such a blessing to see this outpouring of the Holy Spirit on the Hispanic people, and to be a small part of this revival of God.

We continued traveling eastward towards New York, and were able to stop in the town I had grown up in, Akron, Ohio. It was fun taking the children to see the house I lived in as a teenager, and to visit my old high school. The kids got a real kick out of it. We stopped to preach at the church we had preached at before in Lancaster, Pennsylvania. An interesting thing happened while we were there. We had just enough money to get there and get a hotel room. We had enough for an inexpensive supper, and that left us eight dollars for the next day. We had a service that night, but a whole day to feed the children on just eight dollars. We didn't know if the church would give us a cash offering or a check. We prayed, because if it was a check, we would not be able to continue on. We had no credit card, and had checked out of the hotel that morning. Hotels require you pay cash when you check in if you don't have a credit card. How would we pay if they gave us a check? We prayed, knowing God had provided for us so far, and we were in His hands. We stretched those eight dollars to feed the children the next day. By the evening service, we were all hungry, not having had any dinner yet. As we sat in the service, little Sharon leaned over and whispered to me that she was hungry and asked if we were going to have dinner after church. She knew we had used the last money for lunch. I assured her God had not forgotten us, He would provide, and yes, we would eat dinner after the service. It seems a sister sitting behind us overheard Sharon.

We had made it a ministry policy to trust God and not ask for money in the churches. We did have cassettes for sale, and books, but we only charged three dollars for the cassettes and five dollars for the books. We often gave away as many as we sold. I had become so disenchanted with the American ministries that spent so much of their time asking for money. Sergio and I felt that if God was leading us,

He would provide. We decided early on that if the day came that we had to ask for money, it was time to quit. Now, I'm not saying that everyone that asks for donations are not in genuine need, or that they aren't operating in faith. There are circumstances where God leads you to take up an offering, but we were ministering among poorer people, and our faith and commitment to the Lord from the beginning was that if He called us, He would provide. God had always blessed us for making our ministry about Him and not about money. We had no doubt that He would continue to provide. We knew if the day came that He did not, it was our cue that He was changing the direction He wanted us to go, or that we had somehow missed the leading of God.

The sister who overheard our daughter ask if we were going to eat dinner must have gone to the pastor to inform him that we had no money and that we had not had dinner that night. God moved mightily in the service, and there were several new lives for Christ. At the end of the service, the pastor got up and said he wanted to take up a special offering for our ministry. He asked the people to be generous, because he wanted to give us a cash offering to bless us. He stated that he was so impressed that we had not asked for anything to come and preach, but that he knew there were many expenses involved in a traveling ministry. He was so tactful, and so sincere. The people responded generously. When we left, we had enough to go to supper, pay another night in the hotel, and continue on our trip to New York. God is so faithful!

Before long, we were back in the New York City area. We stayed with our beloved friends, who had received us the year before. This time, we preached on the radio several times, and doors opened to preach in many other churches. We went to the retreat of the church we had visited in Elizabeth, New Jersey. The church that danced and praised the Lord, that had been such a blessing to us, had us go and preach at their annual retreat in New York, about 4 hours upstate. It was an amazing time. God refreshed us all. We saw God move in prophecy and in power while we were there. We felt so much love among the people. We met a few people from a sister church of theirs from Providence, Rhode Island, which opened the doors for us to go and preach there. I was 8 months pregnant by then.

We had an absolutely wonderful experience in Providence. This church was a large church, much like the church in Elizabeth, where they praised the Lord for hours, with dancing and rejoicing. It was such a blessing. When we returned to New York, I visited a doctor who informed me that it appeared the baby would come early and that I should limit my traveling. We had an ultrasound done, and according to that, I was due in early September, but since this was my 5th child, they said it was very possible the baby would come early. We had planned to drive down to Florida, then fly back to Puerto Rico for the birth, but the doctor advised against it. We didn't have any insurance, and no home in the area. Our dear friends, the Escobar family, told us to stay with them for the birth of our baby. We had some medical friends who agreed to come and deliver our baby at home. So, we decided to stay and wait.

Our Television program "Encuentro de Amistad"
(left to right) with co-host Jose La Torre, Charlene and Sergio

CHAPTER FIFTEEN
"A great trial, A great blessing"

And so the wait began, and weeks turned into a month. They had said the baby would come early, but the due date came and went. I began to think there was a error in reading the ultrasound, so I called to ask if it was possible that there was a mistake. They asked me why, (supposing I had delivered weeks earlier), but became very alarmed when I told them I was STILL pregnant. They advised me to go immediately to a hospital, as something had to be wrong, but I knew there was nothing wrong, and God gave me a peace to continue to wait on Him. The days went by slowly. I was so large I could no longer bend or do much of anything. I looked like I was having triplets! The baby had dropped and was resting on my pelvic bone. There was so much discomfort, I found it difficult to dress myself or to sleep at night. I went every week to our Doctor friend and they would check me at their house. The progress was minimal.

While we were waiting for the baby to come, news came over the air of a large hurricane that was approaching. It was headed straight for Puerto Rico and it was upgraded to a category five. We prayed and waited, remembering the warning and the vision God had given me. The storm hit the island with great force. Trees and leaves were downed all over the island. Electric lines were out, and many areas were flooded. We could not get through to our family there for days.

Eventually we reached someone who went to check on them. They were well, but the little house we stayed in had lost the roof. Rains continued, and everything inside would have been damaged. We were extremely sad about it, but there was nothing we could do. We were thankful that we were not there when it happened. No one was able to go into the little house to get any of our things out, as the door seemed to be jammed. Eventually a neighbor got a ladder and went in through the ceiling. His report to us was that everything was damaged, except for what was in a metal cabinet. The center beam from the roof had fallen and was laying across the floor, blocking the cabinet from opening and the front door. This beam sealed the cabinet from the winds opening it and blowing everything away. We were marveled, as what was in the cabinet was all the prophetic writings God had given me, along with our family photo albums. God had preserved the most important from being blown away! We heard from Brother Yiye Avila's ministry that great damage had been done to many of the Christian radio and television towers had been damaged, but that his tower suffered no damage at all. They were able to continue broadcasting as soon as electricity was restored in the island! God was sending a message! I wish I could say that the message was received by all, but those who were accusing their brothers, simply stated it was the devil trying to destroy them because they preached the truth. Still, there were those who had heard the warning and repented. Many turned to helping each other out, even though some did not.

There was no way we could return to Puerto Rico to help our family in the clean up. The baby was already past due. I was having contractions that would come and go from time to time. September turned into October. One evening I thought the baby was coming, and the Christian doctor came all the way from Queens to New Jersey with the hopes the baby was coming, only to have the contractions stop around three in the morning. I was so frustrated. Sergio tried to encourage me and comfort me, but it was becoming overwhelming. My body ached continually. I didn't want to complain and worry the children. I remember one evening excusing myself to "take a shower", and went into the bathroom to cry. I couldn't understand why God was letting me go through this. I tried everything but nothing seemed to work. Most mothers reading this will relate to the last few weeks of pregnancy and understand exactly what I mean, but this was not weeks before, but rather, weeks after the due date. Yes, I wanted to just go to a hospital, but I had no insurance. Every time I prayed, God would tell me to be patient and wait. Then there had been two calls, one from Puerto Rico and another from California from two people who didn't know what was going on, saying the Lord had given them a message for sister Charlene. The Lord told both of them the same thing! "There is a time for everything, and the Lord says, it's not time yet." How was I going to ignore this? God had always led me through every step, by His Spirit. Was I going to give in to my screaming flesh, demanding deliverance from this ordeal, or wait on the Lord? I remember becoming so overwhelmed that I cried out to God, "Why have you forgotten me?", then I quickly repented of being angry with Him. I was comforted by His Spirit when He reminded me that Jesus had cried out the same words.

The days continued on. I was supposed to give birth the beginning of September, and now we were in the middle of October! It surely couldn't be much longer, I thought. My stomach was so hard, like it was continually in a contraction. I thought I would explode! Then there was the trips to the store that Sergio would encourage me to go out and get some exercise. People would look at me almost with pity in their eyes, or at least it seemed that way to me. They would ask, "When are you due?" How was I suppose to respond to that? I found it easier to stay at home. I got so tired of friends calling to ask if we had the baby yet, and when I would tell them no, they would say, "NOT YET?" I can't tell you how close I got to giving up and disobeying what the Lord told me to do, which was to wait.

On the 31st of October, I awoke with a song in my Spirit, and God told me the time had come. I was feeling some twinges, and believing the labor was beginning, we were unable to get in touch with our doctor friend, so we called a pastor who called his personal physician and he agreed to see me. When we went to the office, he seemed very concerned, and then told us to go to the hospital, as he didn't hear the baby's heartbeat. Sergio was stressed, to say the least. As we drove towards the nearest hospital, we prayed, and I felt the baby move. I told Sergio not to fear, the baby was alive and well. At the hospital they tried to induce labor, but when they heard I had no insurance, they decided to send us down to Jersey City Hospital, which took charity cases. So off we were sent to Jersey City Medical Center.

We entered this massive hospital structure, filled with people. At that point they checked me, and I was spotting blood, so they sent me straight up to delivery. It was around four in the afternoon. They hooked me up to an ultrasound and said the baby was very large, but believed I would be able to have him. One doctor made fun of me when he asked how far overdue I was, and I told him the due date had been for September. He asked why in the world I would have waited for so long to come in. I told him I was a Christian, and God had told me to wait. He mockingly said, "Well, why didn't you just wait six weeks more, and be pregnant for a full year". He was very cynical, acting like I was some cult follower. He chided me on the dangers of being so far overdue, and left. Labor continued very slowly. Around eight o'clock at night, they decided to break my water, hoping it would make things go more quickly. Unfortunately, the pressure caused the baby to move, and now he was coming with his arm up over his head. They had to hook me back up to the ultrasound and reach up and push him up enough that they could move his arm. In all this, they gave me no medication, but God was with me. They kept saying it was too close to his birth to give me anything, and yet the hours continued on. This same doctor began to take notice of how I praised the Lord quietly even while in such pain. I thanked them even after the procedure of pushing the baby back up to rearrange him, to which he surprisingly asked me why I was thanking them. I told him and the nurse, "I know you are just trying to help me and my baby."

He left the room rather puzzled. (I often thought perhaps this whole ordeal was for the purpose of this man)

A nurse, who was a Christian came in and from the moment she entered my room, she started praising the Lord. She said, "Sister, I don't know who you are, but the Glory of God is all over you. God is here with you!" I knew He was with me, because I had such a peace, even if I was in pain. I would hear others crying out in pain, and I would pray for them. There was a fourteen year old girl brought in that was screaming in pain. I prayed particularly for her. Sergio was by my side for the whole ordeal. He took such good care of me! I could see how worried he was, and so I tried to keep myself calm and composed so as not to make it worse for him. We prayed together off and on as the hours wore on. Around midnight, the Christian nurse came to let us know her shift was over but that the Lord had given her a word for me: "Sorrow lasts for the night, but joy comes in the morning." I thanked her and continued through my ordeal. The doctor left as well, and a female physician took his place.

Somewhere around three in the morning, I began to feel extremely weak. I hadn't eaten since lunch, but it was more than that. I couldn't even lift my head. My voice became weak, and I felt as if I were going to pass out. I whispered to Sergio that I had no more strength. He ran out to look for a doctor but found no one. When he returned, he was very alarmed, as he said I was as white as a sheet. I began praying quietly, and he fell out on the floor to intercede for my life. (He said it was as if he could see the life ebbing out of me). I remember telling the Lord I was ready to go with Him, if it was His will, but I had the children who needed me, and Sergio, plus there were so many things He had told me He was going to do in my life that hadn't been fulfilled yet. I remember telling Him to do His will, and then I quoted this scripture from the Word of God, "I can do all things through Christ who strengthens me." Sergio said he was on the floor praying when he heard me quote that scripture out loud. Within minutes my blood pressure (that had gone way up) came back down to normal, and the color returned to my face. I was able to lift my head and felt strengthened. The doctor came in and checked and told me it was time to wheel me into the delivery room.

The doctor told me later that there were several reasons why she should have taken the baby but she kept feeling that I was able to have the baby naturally. I was still not sure how I was going to find the strength to push this baby out. I remember the doctor saying if she had to, she would get on my stomach and help me push it out. Strange thing to hear! Anyway, when she finally told me to push, I pushed with all my strength, and then I felt something come over me, and this force pushed even harder. It was like a car hitting overdrive! Sounds silly, but that's the only thing I can say. From nowhere, this strength came over me with every contraction. I gave birth to Benjamin Isaac Ramirez at six in the morning, as the sun was first coming up! He was ten pounds and 12 ounces, and twenty four inches long! He was a beautiful, healthy baby! It was the largest baby the doctor had delivered to that point. Sergio took him and dedicated him to the Lord, as he did with our other children. What a beautiful child, from the moment he was born!

The trial was over. I was exhausted but overjoyed. They put me in a recovery room where I got to share Jesus with the fourteen year old girl who had been brought in to deliver her baby! The male doctor, who had mocked me the day before, saw me in the recovery room and stopped to speak to me. I was very surprised when he affectionately took my hand and turned to some of the interns that were accompanying him and said, "This woman is a marvel. We put her through so much last night, and she never made a sound. In fact, she thanked us for helping her!" I could see the sincerity in his eyes. I realized then that God had touched him through what had happened. He asked me what I had, a boy or girl, and how we both were doing. He told me he hoped to get up and see me later on. I was totally shocked at the change in his demeanor. I want to state how important it is to live our faith in every moment of our life, because you just never know who is watching, and what the Lord can do through a servant who is obedient and praises their Lord through every thing.

Sergio was exhausted after being up with me all night. He went back to the house to tell the children they had a baby brother. The experience had been completely overwhelming for him as well. He was thinking seriously about being operated on so he would never have to see me go through anything like that again. When he came back to the hospital that afternoon he told me he had gone to speak with someone about a vasectomy. Now, let me tell you, after you have just gone through having a baby, the last thing you want to think about is having more children. But years earlier when I had prayed about marrying Sergio, God told me we would have four children. When we had David and Sharon, I already had Chad and Christian, so that made four, or so I thought at the time. But when I became pregnant with Benjamin, I knew God was saying Sergio and I would have four, and Benjamin was number three. As much as I wasn't wanting to go through something like that ever again, I knew what the Lord had said. I tried to convince Sergio, but he said he almost lost me, and he couldn't bare that, so he was going to at least check into it. As he went down to his meeting with a counselor there in the hospital, I prayed for God to do His will. He came back up later and told me the counselor was a Christian, and she told him she felt he was making a decision while under a great deal of emotional distress. She wanted him to take some time to think about it and pray about it, and did not set him up for any appointment. I told him what I had prayed, and he decided to put it on hold and wait on the Lord.

Two days later we took Benny home to the Escobar's house to meet his new brothers and sister. It was love at first sight for all. Benny was a smiley baby. He never cried. He was strong, and was able to lift his head by himself from the very beginning (no wonder, he was actually like a six week old baby when he was born). A pediatrician examined him, stating that babies born that late often have health problems or disabilities, but all they could tell us was that he had a big head, a big body, a big liver and lungs, because he was a big baby! Sergio's comment to me was, "and they go all those years to school to be able to make that diagnosis?" We found it extremely comical.

So, we didn't have Benny at home, but at one of the biggest hospitals I had ever seen. You could see the Statue of Liberty from the window. We were concerned about how much it would cost. When the bill arrived, it was for seven thousand dollars! They charged me for using the delivery room, and then they sent a bill in Benjamin's name, charging HIM for using the delivery room as well! How in the world were we going to pay such a bill? We went to the hospital's financial office to discuss the matter, and to our amazement, there was a special program they informed us that we might be eligible for, so we applied. Within weeks we were approved, and the entire hospital bill was covered! God had provided, once again!

In El Paso, meeting the Vergara family for the first time
(left to right) Lalo Vergara, Charlene, Marisela, Lily,
baby Benny, Christian
Sharon, David, Gabriela, and Sergio Vergara

CHAPTER SIXTEEN
"Western doors open"

Life totally changed with the arrival of baby Benjamin, or Benny, as we called him. We presented him to the Lord at the church in Elizabeth, New Jersey, when he was eight days old. The most amazing thing was when the pastor was about to pray, he asked the congregation to stretch their hands out towards us, and join in prayer, and little Benny raised his arm in the air, and kept it held there throughout the prayer. We were all amazed at this. We knew God had placed His hand on this new little addition to our family.

Traveling and preaching was difficult, to say the least, with children, let alone a new baby. We returned back to Puerto Rico when Benny was a few weeks old. Our little house in the Rain forest, had been damaged from Hugo, but FEMA had approved help to repair the house. We stayed in the big house with Sergio's parents, who were delighted to meet the new grandson. (My parents had come to see him when we were in the hospital in New Jersey). My in-laws loved babies! They were disappointed when we couldn't fly back to have the baby as we had originally planned, but they understood, and they were very glad that we hadn't done so, as we would have been in the middle of the hurricane. They had spent weeks after without electricity or water. God had kept us and our baby safely out of harms way.

As I said before, Benjamin rarely cried, but then, he always had someone around to pick him up right away! Sharon, who had wanted a baby sister, was delighted there was a baby in the house, regardless of the fact it was another boy. She was such a little mother, so I had a lot of help. When we went to preach, we took the children with us as much as possible, but with the new baby, we often had to have Christian take care of them. Christian was excellent with his brother and sister, and now with the baby as well. He absolutely loved the baby, and it was mutual. David would make him chuckle so loud that it made us all laugh. Sergio was on cloud nine, having another little baby to hold. Before long, we couldn't imagine what life was like without that little boy in our lives.

God always provided for our family. At Christmas time that year, Sharon told us she wanted a special doll she had seen advertised on television while we were in the States. It was a strange, large headed doll with a furry face called a "Huggins Doll". They had several different kinds, but she wanted the one with the purple hair. We looked all over Puerto Rico for the doll, but it had not come to the island yet. As Christmas drew nearer, we kept asking her what else she wanted, but she kept saying all she wanted was her "Huggins doll". Not wanting to see her disappointed on Christmas morning, we prayed to the Lord. We told her only the Lord could bring her that doll, as we had looked everywhere and couldn't find one in Puerto Rico. She prayed!

Two days before Christmas we went to the mall once again to check all the stores, only to come up empty handed again. We went to the car, and I remembered I had forgotten to get something we needed for baby Benny from the pharmacy. Everyone was tired, so Sergio told me he would wait in the car with the children while I ran back into the Walgreens in the mall. Now, everyone knows that the toy section in a Walgreens is very limited, and we hadn't found the doll, not even in the toy stores. I went to get what I needed for Benny and headed down an aisle towards the cash register. It was a medicine aisle. Suddenly, the Lord spoke to me and told me to stop and look up. On the very top of the shelf was the purple Huggins doll! There was only one! It was the very one she wanted! There were no other toys on the shelf, and I had already checked the toy section and there was none there. I knew it was a miracle from the Lord! I bought some black trash bags so I could hide the doll in one of them, and took it to the car. I could hardly contain my excitement. Sergio was rather surprised to see me lugging this large black plastic bag, and of course he asked me. I didn't want Sharon to hear, so I told him in Spanish, "I found her doll!"

On Christmas morning we could hardly wait for her to open her special gift from the Lord. When she opened it her eyes got big. She began to thank the Lord for answering her prayer. It was a precious moment. (Several years later, the Lord reminded me of this incident. I was praying and telling Him how anxious I was to see Him, when He asked me if I remembered how anxious I had been to see Sharon's face that Christmas morning. Of course I remembered, I told Him, and He replied that was how He anticipates the moment when we, His children, get to see Him face to face. He desires to see the look of pure joy on our faces when we look upon Him for the first time.)

When Benny was about six months old, we were called to return to preach in the United States. We returned once again, this time with a baby as well. Before we left, an evangelist from Yiye Avila's ministry spoke with us and gave us the name and number of a Christian brother in Juarez, Mexico, who had coordinated several services for him in Mexico and El Paso. We called this brother, Eduardo Vergara, or Lalo, as he preferred to be called. He was delighted to work with us. We gave him the dates we would be going through El Paso, and he went to work. When we arrived to El Paso, he came and met us at our hotel. He had a full two weeks of services set up for us. He came with his wife, Maricela, and his three children, Lily, Sergio, and Gabriela. The children were delighted to meet other children. We quickly made great friends with this lovely family. His daughter Lily was a lovely young girl, about seventeen at the time. Christian had just turned fourteen, but he was a very mature young man. Over the next few days as we spent a great deal of time together, I began to notice how Christian and Lily were looking at each other. They spent a great deal of time play "fighting" over which one would hold the baby, and which one of them he wanted to be with.

Lalo took us to the Christian Television Station in El Paso, KSCE-TV. They were having a board meeting, and he felt he should take Sergio there. At the meeting, they felt led to ask Sergio to pray. Later a board member came to him and told him that he felt God had a purpose in sending us there. We soon made friends with the station General Manager, Grace Rendall, and she was interested in carrying our program that we taped at Yiye's ministry in Puerto Rico. We were on the air on a program that they held mid-day, a talk show and prayer program. We already had services scheduled in Los Angeles, but we agreed to come back to help with a telethon the station was going to have, and to contact Jose La Torre, who was the host of our program to see how we could begin sending tapes of our program in Puerto Rico to El Paso. At the end of the two weeks, it was obvious to me that something was beginning to develop. It was hard for us to leave for California after we had made so many new friends and seen the great need across the border in Juarez. It was also hard for the children as they had gotten rather attached to Lalo's children, especially, Christian and Lily.

We preached at some of the same churches we first preached in when we reached Los Angeles, but we were also interviewed on radio and Spanish Christian television there. Doors seemed to open more than the first time. We stayed with the same deacon, Hector Lugo, where we stayed the first time for several weeks. He had some more family come to stay, so we were delighted when the door opened for us to stay with another family in Venice Beach. The children really enjoyed it when we stayed in California. There was so much to see and do out there, in between the services we had, but Christian was anxious for us to return to El Paso. We took the children to Six Flags, and they had a ball! We went to the beach, and went site-seeing. We tried to include fun things for them, as they "went to work" with the parents on such a continual basis.

We had also been invited to preach in San Francisco. God gave me a message, a warning for that city, and then he opened the doors for us to go and deliver it. It was our first trip to San Francisco, so it was a new adventure for all of us. While it is a beautiful city, with so much to do and see, it is a very sinful city as well, very liberal, very cosmopolitan. We saw some things that I hadn't seen anywhere else, same sex "couples" around the city, displaying inappropriate affection, and several churches of Satan. We actually preached in a Pentecostal church a half a block from one of these Satanic churches. The oppression in the city was something I had never encountered before, not even in New York City, where I had seen teen prostitutes in the streets at night, and pornographic stores and theaters. This was a whole other level of evil. The sad thing is to see the young teens all drugged up headed into these churches. The church was painted black on the outside, with a large "S" painted in red on the front. These churches were listed in the yellow pages under "churches" as if they were just another religious group! I wondered how far down this city, and our country for that matter, could go. I was certain that freedom of religion that our founding fathers set forth for us all was not meant to cover this. I understood why the message from the Lord was so harsh.

It was a difficult time, a time where we prayed a great deal. I was told that new churches would pop up (Spanish) and struggled, but never grew much. Many of them didn't last long. Christians told me there was a great oppression in that city, and now I understood it. It was a blessing to be able to minister and encourage our brothers and sisters who live under this oppression. Still, we were delighted to leave, and we carried a burden away with us for this city and for the body of Christ that lives there.

We were able to take a side trip on our way back through Yosemite National Park and it was awesome! We had left a city that was depraved in many ways, yet beautiful none the less, and there before us was the grandeur and beauty of the Lord's creation! I think we needed this time of refreshing after pouring out so much of ourselves in ministering in San Francisco. We traveled through the giant Sequoia trees. It is unbelievable how big those trees are! The kids had a great time, and baby Benny was an absolute angel. It was a bit crowded traveling in that old Chrysler Newport with four children, but we managed to drive back towards El Paso, Texas, tired but happy.

While we were in California, much to our surprise, child number four was on the way! We had not planned to have another child so soon. Benny was only seven months old when I became pregnant with Joshua. It amazes me as I look back, how I managed to do all these things while pregnant! God certainly is our strength and shield!

When we returned to El Paso, we rented a hotel room on a monthly basis, and prepared to get to work. The kids were delighted to be back with their friends, and we often went to lunch together, or had Lalo's family over to swim in the hotel pool. It was July, so we celebrated David's birthday with a pool party. While standing watching the children, Maricela and I, I suddenly felt the Lord's revealing He had a plan for Christian and Lily together. I remember telling Maricela, but she just laughed, saying they were both way too young, still I couldn't shake the feeling that Lily was God's choice for Christian. He and Lily went to a youth retreat in Juarez, and came back on fire for the Lord. They told us how the Lord had moved at the retreat, and how God had used them both. They were anxious to pray over their siblings and share this "fire" with them. It was a blessing watching them minister to the other children. I could see the bond between them had deepened through this experience.

We helped with the telethon, and signed the contracts to officially become programmers on KSCE. We arranged to tape some programs as well as air some of our tapes from Puerto Rico. The doors continued to open. One day Lalo had two services scheduled in Juarez, one for Sergio in one church, and another one for me at another location. Lalo went with Sergio and Maricela went with me.

As we drove through the city of Juarez, it was easy to see why so many try to cross the border. There are affluent areas, and areas of great poverty. It is a city of extremes. We took a turn and entered a garbage dump. I assumed we were taking a "short cut" to the church. This was an enormous city dump that was blocks long. I noticed that there were families that lived in this dump. They constructed homes from what they found. They had make-shift walls, zinc sheets for roofs, with old tires holding the roof on. They made windows out of oven doors or old refrigerator shelves. It was truly an amazing and humbling site. There was not plumbing or electricity to these homes. They constructed communal outhouses. We came to a block concrete structure in the middle of this dump. It was the only real constructed building there. IT WAS THE CHURCH! They had a generator and a string of light bulbs strung up. I was not prepared for this! I felt so inadequate. How was I suppose to minister to people in this level of poverty? How was I to relate to them? I began to pray, thinking I would find depressed, needy people inside.

To my surprise, when I entered the church, it was filled with people singing and praising God! They danced before the Lord and had such expressions of love and joy on their faces. I was in shock! I remember kneeling down and praying on the concrete floor. My question to the Lord was: "Don't these people know how poor they really are?" Much to my surprise, the Lord answered me; "You see these people? For many Christians, I am one thing in the midst of many things they "have"; but to these people, I am ALL THEY HAVE!" I was so humbled by these words. I began to cry as I looked at their joyful, devoted faces. I told the Lord, "Then we should all be as these people." I had found people who loved the LORD FOR WHO HE IS, not for what He gives them. God healed many there that night, and some who had just come to visit, gave their lives to the Lord. We gave out tapes to anyone who had access to a cassette recorder. (It turns out they would take broken ones they found in the dump and repair them using parts from this one and that one, and that was their only source of entertainment). I had taken about 30 tapes with me, and we gave out tapes to many people, yet when we got back to the motel and counted, we had 27 tapes left! How was that possible? I know we had given away to over 20 people, but there it was! God had multiplied the tapes! (No we didn't just miscount them). Our God is a mighty God!

When we left El Paso, we felt God was leading us to move our ministry to that area. We continued to pray for confirmation as we headed back to Florida. We spent some time with my parents before returning back to Puerto Rico. Now we had to tell Sergio's parents that we were going to be spending more time Stateside than in Puerto Rico. They had finished the repairs on the little house, and we were able to stay in our little house again, if only for awhile.

Our life on the road (in the $400.00 car)
(left to right) Christian, David, baby Joshua, Charlene, Benny, and Sharon

CHAPTER SEVENTEEN
"And then there were two babies"

Although God had called us to Puerto Rico, and had used me to bring a warning to the "religious" of the island, more and more I felt God leading us back to the States. Doors had opened so much out west in Texas, and in California. It had been spoken to me by the Lord back in 1989, and this area of the ministry was growing rapidly, while at the same time, the doors were not as open in Puerto Rico. We did minister through Yiye's ministry, via television, but times were changing. The Evangelist Jose La Torre, with whom we had the television program on the air in Puerto Rico, left the ministry and moved to Florida. The program in Puerto Rico was no more, but the program in El Paso continued. We knew we needed to be there in order to continue to tape programs. When we were there, we had taped several weeks of programs, but now we didn't have any from Puerto Rico to send them. We returned to El Paso, entering on the night that Operation Dessert Storm began in Kuwait, January of 1991.

El Paso, Texas is home to Fort Bliss, a major Army military base. We found a house to rent and many Christians supplied furniture and items to help us get started. We put the children in public school for the first time in a long time. I stayed home with Benny, who was now one, and awaited the arrival of our next baby in March. Sharon did not do well in public school. She was very sad being away from her mother and dad. She came home to tell us that many of the children in her second grade class had mommies and daddies that went off to war, and the children would cry in class. She was very concerned about this. God spoke a word to Sergio that if His people, if the churches would join together and pray in faith for our soldiers, God would bring them all back alive. He spoke this word over our television program and over the radio. Several pastors thought it was not from God, and that we were getting peoples hopes up falsely, but Sergio was certain it was the Lord, and so was I, so we stood by the word God had given. Sharon told the children in school what her daddy said God had said. She told them to pray and God would bring their mommies and daddies back safely.

One day the teacher called us and told us she thought we should put Sharon back in home school as she would cry every day. We asked her why she hadn't told us she didn't like school, and she said she just missed us so much, but she didn't want to worry us. She was always that way. She never wanted to worry us and she never asked for things like most children do. We decided to put her back in home school and let her help me with her baby brother and the new baby that was soon coming.

Lalo had Christian friends who were doctors. They had opened a clinic in Juarez, and so he arranged for them to give me a check up. They ran several tests and told me all was well with my baby and gave us a due date of March 1st. We were more than welcomed to go and have the baby at the clinic, but we were concerned about the problems that might cause as far as citizenship, so one of the doctors said he agreed, and he would be more than happy to go to our home in El Paso to deliver the baby. We went back and forth for weekly check ups. Some sisters from different churches got together and had a baby shower for me. God provided everything we needed for our new arrival.

I was concerned I would be late again, like I had been with Benny, but God assured me that this time it would be different. He had shown me with the birth of Benny there was a purpose. While He did not tell me this during that long ordeal, weeks after Benny was born, God explained the reason. He told me how I had been told that Benjamin would come early, and I believed it. I had all the signs and symptoms to confirm it, but it did not happen the way I was told, or how I believed. It had not been easy, painless, as it had been with the birth of Sharon. Then He explained to me why: He reminded me how He had once told me He would take me through things that His people would go through, ahead of time, so that I would be able to minister to them. He said that many in the body of Christ have been told that when times get hard, in the end times, they would be taken in the rapture. Many were not preparing to endure trials and hardships, because they felt they would not ever go through any of it. Then the Lord reminded me of the parable of the bridegroom who came for the bride at midnight; when does a wedding ever begin at midnight? In other words, the wedding didn't start at a normal time, it started much later than expected. Some brides didn't have enough oil for their lamps, because they didn't expect they would need it. In the same way, many are not preparing to "wait" on the Lord until He comes. They are not preparing to "go the distance" if necessary. When stressful times come, if they do, will they have the faith to hang on and remain faithful until He returns? This was the lesson of the trial of Benjamin's birth, but this was not going to be the issue with this delivery.

On March the 2nd, one day after my due date, in the early hours of the morning, the contractions began. Sergio called the doctor, and he came from Juarez. It was not a quick delivery, but it was not extremely painful either. The pain seemed to be centered in my back this time. I found it easier to be up walking around. The only thing that seemed to help was standing in the shower, so I took a lot of hot showers that day. I would stay there until the hot water ran out. Things progressed throughout the day, but began to slow down in the late afternoon. The doctor, Sergio and the children decided to get together to pray as I headed off to the shower to relieve the pain. While I was in the shower, I felt a contraction that was so strong, I went on my knees. Suddenly, the baby was coming out! I called for help, and they came and helped me out of the bathtub. With Sergio on one side and the doctor on the other, they walked me down the hall to our room. I kept telling them the baby was coming NOW! Once we reached the room and the doctor checked, he verified that I was indeed correct! With a few more contractions, our baby was born. The doctor said he was born with the cord wrapped around his neck two times! That was the reason the delivery was prolonged. The doctor quickly unwrapped the cord, and checked the baby. He was just fine! He told us that amazingly, the cord was over twice as long as a normal cord. He had no doubt that God had given our baby an "extension cord" in order for him to be born without any damage to him. God is faithful!

We had this beautiful little baby boy, well, not so little. He weighed nine pounds, seven ounces. Sharon went with her dad to help him clean up the baby, and David helped me to the shower to clean up. They were both so touched being there present for the birth of their brother. Christian was caring for Benny. (They have told me through the years how much it helped them to appreciate what their mother had done in order to give birth to them.) We named him Joshua Elias (Elijah). So now we had two in diapers in the house!

The two little ones came to be known as "the babies". We took them along with the children to all the services we had. We would pull out our playpen and set it up in the back of the church. I heard a testimony a sister gave once. She had three children and was battling with the Lord about serving Him, with the excuse that she had these three little children to care for. She said when she saw me with five children, and two of them just babies, go and preach, God spoke to her and asked her if I was able to do it, why wasn't she. She surrendered to God and entered into the ministry with her husband. (She had not accompanied him previously). It turned out to be a great blessing to her and her family. I was glad that I was an inspiration to her. It never occurred to me to stop serving the Lord and preaching His word because of having children. I saw them as God's blessing to me for being faithful, which encouraged me to continue on out of gratitude for these wonderful blessings. Was it difficult at times? Sure, but God deserved so much more than the little I gave. I saw how God intervened in the birth of these children, in the caring for their lives, and in providing for us all, how could I not serve Him? It was a joy to be called to serve Him! It was never a job, or a burden. I saw it as a privilege and an honor.

As we continued to minister over the next few months, the war in Kuwait came to an end with victory. We had seen the city with yellow ribbons all over, a moving testimony to the prayers and support of a community. So many families had someone over there. I remember the miles and miles of train cars with military vehicles being sent over to Kuwait, when the war started, along with so many soldiers who were sent from Fort Bliss. It was a wonderful day in May of 1991 when the war ended and the soldiers came back to El Paso. As God had spoken, all of the soldiers who had fought in Kuwait from El Paso came back. We saw the ceremony live over television when they returned home. Every one of the soldiers were present and accounted for! Praise God! Those who had been skeptical of the word God had given my husband had to acknowledge that the word had truly been from the Lord. It was beautiful to see so many people show up at the airport to welcome the soldiers back home. Some held up signs inviting a soldier to "Come Home with us", for those soldiers who didn't have family there to receive them. It was a time of tears and rejoicing for us all.

By the time July came, we had taped a lot of programs, the doors were opening in California once again, and we felt led to put our things in storage and head to California. We knew we would spend time going back and forth between El Paso and Los Angeles. We were now traveling, but staying in a certain location for a few months before moving on. It was time to "move on" to Los Angeles.

CHAPTER EIGHTEEN
"The loss of loved ones"

We were back in California again. The Aranda family received us in their home in Bell Gardens, and we began preaching throughout the city. New doors opened each week. We returned to preach on HCCN Christian Latin Television. God moved mightily in the services. In one of the services we had, a Christian man, who had been in one of our services in the past, approached us and told us what a blessing our ministry had been in his life. He started going to all of our services. Before long, he started helping us with coordinating services. His name was Cuahtemoc Barcelo. Hector Lugo was having health issues and could not help out as much, and so having Cuahtemoch to help us was a great blessing. Our children became great friends with the Aranda's children. As the doors opened more and more, we began to realize that it was too difficult to stay with people for such a long time, so we began thinking and planning for our next trip, to rent an apartment and stay longer.

After we had preached in Los Angeles for a few weeks, doors opened for us to go and preach in San Francisco, so we scheduled it into a space of time we didn't have any services scheduled in LA. We arrived and took a hotel room for the weekend. The children weren't feeling very well. We thought it was a flu, but soon they began to breakout with a rash, especially Christian and David. Benjamin had it too, but not too bad. Sharon and Joshua had a little bit of fever, but only a couple of bumps appeared on them. It was chickenpox! We had a four day crusade planned, and so we took turns going to preach and caring for sick children. If that wasn't enough, we received a call from Cuahtemoc to call Puerto Rico. Sergio's brother, Luis, had passed away. He was a Vietnam veteran who had lost both his legs over there. He was only forty two years old. We were not surprised, as his health had deteriorated over the last few months. He had a serious drinking problem. As much as we tried to reach him, he would just push us away. His liver had failed and he was hospitalized. Sergio's mother told us that before he slipped into a coma, he had given his life to Christ. The sorrow we felt was comforted by the fact that he had given his life to Christ, and we would one day see him again. We were very concerned about Sergio's parents, but we had five sick children. How were we going to fly back for the funeral? We discussed it and I told Sergio to go, but he didn't want to leave me with five sick children, two of them being babies. On top of all of this, his parents car had blown the engine, and they had no way to get around. After discussing it with them, we decided to send them the little money we had that we would use for the airfare so that they could buy a car. They agreed as they were stuck out in the country without any way to get around. We couldn't bring his brother back, but we could help them. It was a very hard time for us all, especially for Sergio, but we planned to return as quickly as possible, as soon as we raised enough for the airfare to return to be with his parents.

We finally returned to Puerto Rico to see Sergio's family. Sergio's mother was not doing well. We stayed in our little house, which had been rebuilt from the damage from Hugo. We spent days caring for my ailing mother-in-law. She had a tumor which grew in her brain, and she was no longer able to get around or speak well. They attempted a surgery, with no guarantees, and unfortunately, the surgery left her unable to speak at all. The tumor was wrapped around a part of her brain and it was just a matter of time. The death of Luis had affected her tremendously, and she seemed to no longer have the will to live. It was a difficult time for us all, but we felt it was important to be there for her. She would often cry and would not be consoled. They kept asking her if she was in pain, but she would just shake her head and put her hand over her chest. I asked her if she wanted to go home to be with Jesus, and she nodded. She was heartbroken and she didn't want to live her final days like that. We prayed that the Lord would heal her or take her home. She seemed to find some comfort when Sergio would sit with her. She would smile and "pet" Sergio, as he sat beside her. When she became too ill, she was moved to a hospital, where they could keep her medicated. He and his dad went every day to see her.

In May, we were invited to preach a crusade at the church in Elizabeth, NJ. Sergio's mom was real bad, and I hesitated to accept the invitation. We prayed about it and discussed it. We couldn't leave her now, plus we didn't have the money for us all to fly there. God had it planned. I would go and Christian would go with me, and Sergio would stay with the rest of the children and care for them and for his mom. It would be the first time we would be separated or that I would go to minister on my own, but God confirmed it, so I purchased the airfare. Christian and I flew in on a Thursday with a return ticket for the following Tuesday. The services were spectacular! I have never felt the power of God so intense as I did in these services. On the second evening, the presence of God came down in that place so intense that all we could do was to fall down on the ground and worship Him. The altars filled each night with lives for Christ, and many were healed when we prayed for the sick. It was amazing! In the midst of this, on Sunday I received a call from Sergio that his mother had passed away.

On Sunday morning, Joshua was not feeling well, so Sergio's dad went by himself to the nursing home. When he arrived, they had her sitting in a wheel chair. She seemed to be better! She spoke for the first time in weeks, telling him she was going with "El Señor", which has two meanings, it can refer to "the man" but it is also used to say "the Lord". He didn't understand and kept telling her she wasn't going anywhere with any man, she had to stay there. About a half hour later she was gone. He didn't realize until then that she was trying to tell him that she was going with Jesus to her heavenly home. While it was very sad to hear the news of her passing, the miracle of her speaking, and the message she gave, was comforting. We knew the Lord had taken her. I was beside myself, as I was not there to be with them, but the ticket was not changeable. Monday was such a long day, and we were glad when we got on the plane to head back to Puerto Rico. The viewing was Tuesday afternoon, and we landed at the airport and went straight to the Funeral home.

The next few weeks were a healing time for the family, especially for my father-in-law. He knew we needed to get back to work, and did not want to go with us. Sergio's oldest brother, Frank, had not been able to make it down for the funeral, but had plans to come and spend some time with his dad. We reluctantly prepared to return stateside. We had few doors open to us in Puerto Rico. The legalism issue had returned, and God was leading us to leave the island. It hurt to leave his dad there alone, but we needed to follow the leading of the Lord.

We returned to Florida and stayed with my sister for a couple of weeks while we preached at a few churches in the area. My sister, Gail, decided to go with me to one of the services. I was surprised that she wanted to go along, but very delighted. I told her I would be speaking in Spanish, but she said that was something she really wanted to see. She remembered me as a weak, frightened, highly imaginative, very sensitive girl, and she found the change in my life so surprising that she wanted to see for herself. I had told her how God had given me the ability to speak in Spanish, and I think she was a little skeptical. She had learned a little more of the language when we were in Peru as children, and had taken it in high school as well, so she thought she would be able to understand to some extent.

I have to admit, it made me very nervous taking her with me, but I was hoping the Lord would touch her and she would finally give her life to the Lord. The service was in an auditorium where this church met for services. I prayed intensly before the service, but once I was up on the stage and at the pulpit, the nervousness left me. I focused on the message and tried to avoid looking at my sister. The Lord moved in the service, and you could just feel His presence. At the end, I gave an altar call, and prayed for the lives which came forward. My sister was not one of them, but on the way home she told me she was actually blown away with it all. She said she couldn't believe it was her "little sister" up there in front of all those people. When she heard me speaking in Spanish, she realized that it was truly miraculous, as she KNEW I was not fluent like that before. She told me even though she didn't understand everthing I said, she was so touched by being there and by what God had done in my life. At the time of the altar call she hadn't gone forward, but she wanted me to know that she did pray. She told the Lord, "Okay, God, you've got my attention. You must be real if you can change someone this much. I'm going to give this a try".

Her daughter, Lisa, had been going to church with some neighborhood children for awhile, and had told me how sad it made her that her mom and dad didn't go to church with her. I had prayed with my niece about this for serveral years, and from seeing the testimony of what the Lord had done in my life, my sister finally came to Christ and started to go to church with her daughter! Before long, my brother-in-law and my nephew started going to church as well, and the whole family came to Christ! God had made a promise to me years before when I was in Lafayette, that He would save my family, and it was such a blessing to see His faithfulness!

We also had an opportunity to preach in a church near Homestead. While we were there, God gave me a vision of a great hurricane that positioned itself over top of south Florida. The damage it caused was enormous. The Lord spoke a word to the congregation telling them to enter a month of prayer and repentance. He said that surely this storm would come, but if they would be obedient, He would protect them and the church and that not a drop of water would damage the church. It was a strange word, but I knew it was the Lord. The people were very touched, and the pastor called for a month of prayer. Six weeks later, hurricane Andrew hit south Florida. The devastation to the Homestead area was compared to a bomb exploding. The news was covered with images of entire neighborhoods destroyed. It was like that for the entire neighborhood around this church, but the church itself was untouched. As the Lord spoke, not even a drop of water entered or damaged the church. They had an outside small building that housed a kitchen area and storage, that was blown away, but the church had no damage whatsoever! It was amazing. The church testified to the hand of God, and what God had spoken to them. Each night the church filled with people who came to the Lord due to this testimony. None of the members of the congregation suffered any damage to their homes either. When FEMA came, they couldn't explain why the church stood, but because the other small building was destroyed, the received a check with which they were able to build a brand new church structure that could accommodate all the new people who had come. For them, Andrew turned out to be a great blessing!

By then, my dear brother and sister, Ron and Jean Breaux, who I had living next to me years before in Lafayette, returned and opened a church in Lafayette. We were invited to preach at their church. It was such a blessing to be there with them. It was a very emotional time, as we reminisced over how God had moved and done so many great things in all of our lives. It was the first time they saw Christian since the day they had prayed for him in the hospital. Christian was now a teenager. It was a blessing when he introduced us to the church and told them he wanted them to meet his "first sheep". He told them how proud he was of me as my "spiritual father", and I was very moved. It was always wonderful being back with our old friends, but we had work to do in El Paso. We visited churches in Houston and San Antonio as we traveled westward again.

In El Paso, we were soon back at work taping programs for our television program. The program was such a blessing. It was seen in the El Paso area as well as into Mexico. We had so many testimonies of lives touched by the Lord through the program. One of the most amazing testimonies was from a young woman who wrote to tell us she had been pregnant and was going to have an abortion the next day. She said she was in a lot of turmoil about it and started "channel surfing". When she came to the Christian station, she saw us on the screen, and immediately, Sergio had a word for someone watching. The word was, "you are thinking on having an abortion, but the Lord wants you to know He has plans for the child, and your child will be a great blessing to you." She said she couldn't believe her ears. She knew God was speaking to her, so she canceled her appointment and decided to have her baby. She said her little girl was born and indeed the child was a great blessing in her life and she just wanted to write and thank us for letting God use us to touch people's lives. We received letters of people who were saved, healed, marriages saved, so many wonderful things the Lord allowed us to be a part of. We would always pray before each program we taped, and surrender to whatever the Lord wanted said and done. We felt it was important to yield to God and let the Holy Spirit move. The Lord often had prophetic messages to the audience as well as words of knowledge concerning healing. God is always waiting to move and minister to His people. The secret is for us to get out of His way and let Him do it. That was always the main focus for our program. We didn't need to ask for money to help us pay for the program. People sent offerings, as they were blessed by the Lord, and we were able to pay for the air time.

CHAPTER NINTEEN
"A home on wheels"

Our coordinator in Los Angeles, Cuahtemoc, told us he had services set up for us in Los Angeles in October, but it was now September. We had services in El Paso, plus the programs to tape but we didn't have the funds to pay for the hotel for more than a couple of weeks. A sister (who was a pastor), heard we were back in town and insisted we go and stay with her. We were reluctant to go and stay a full month in someone's home, but she was very insistent, and so we did. While I am grateful for her offering her home, it did not turn out well for us. Her way of doing things and our way were not compatible. We offered to move back to the hotel, but she wouldn't hear of it. Not wanting to offend her any further, we stayed, and counted the days until we would leave for Los Angeles. By this time, it was very tight trying to travel back and forth with four children in a Chrysler Newport. We prayed for the Lord to provide us another vehicle. There were times when our "nomad" lifestyle became over whelming. After staying in this sister's home, it became even more overwhelming. We prayed that God would provide us a home so that we would not have to stay with people any more.

God answered the prayer in a most peculiar way. We received a letter from a viewer stating that they had a gift for us, and asked if we could call them. These dear servants of God had a Toyota trailer home that they wanted to GIVE us! They had purchased it only a few months earlier with the hopes of traveling after he retired, but he developed serious health issues and the trailer was just sitting in their backyard. We couldn't believe our eyes or ears! They handed us the title and the keys and said it was ours! They had been so blessed by our program, and they heard us say we were praying for another vehicle. They weren't sure if that was the kind of vehicle we had in mind, but it was ours if we wanted it. Sergio said he had prayed for a home, and God gave us one with wheels, so he took it we were to continue on the road. The kids were ecstatic. The trailer had an overhead sleeping compartment, a bathroom, stove and refrigerator, and a seating area with a table that converted into a large bed as well. No more cramped back seat! They could travel comfortably and continue their school work at the table. It was such a blessing to us!

We left El Paso in our new home, praising God all the way! We sang songs and played games until late that evening. When the children had finally fallen asleep, and I was laying down with the babies, Sergio began talking to the Lord while he was driving. He was thanking God for such a great blessing. As he thought on it, he remembered how we had sent the money we had saved for a car to his parents when his brother died in order for them to get a car instead. He thought at first that perhaps in giving the money to them instead of using it for our own need, that was the reason why God had given us this new home. The Lord spoke to him and told him that was not the reason. Then God reminded him of an event that had happened several months before.

We were in El Paso and had eaten dinner at a local restaurant. We had leftovers that we took out the door with us. As we headed to our car, a young Mexican man, approached us and said he was hungry. Sergio gave him the bag with food we had and gave him some cash. The young man grabbed a roll from the bag and began to eat it eagerly. He asked if we had a blanket he could cover up with. It was beginning to rain, so Sergio told us to get in the car, while he searched through the trunk for anything, but we had unloaded everything at the hotel. He returned to tell the young man we didn't have a blanket or cover. Then, as we watched from the car, I saw Sergio take off his sweatshirt and put it over the young man's head, helping him to put it on. Sergio stood there in his undershirt speaking to the young man and I told the children to always remember what they just saw their dad do. When Sergio returned shivering to the car, all of us had tears in our eyes. He said he knew he had more warm clothes at the hotel, but this man didn't have anything to keep him warm, so he gave him his clothes. That's just how Sergio is, the most giving man I know. As he spoke to the Lord, the Lord reminded him of this incident and told him, "do you remember this young man? I was there." The scripture says what we do for the least of his brethren, we do for the Lord. Sergio was very touched and told me what the Lord had said once I returned to the front seat with him.

As with most blessings, there are always trials. Somewhere out in the desert that night, on a major interstate, we had a flat tire. Sergio pulled to the side as far as he could get out of the lane of traffic. We had just gotten the vehicle, and we didn't know where anything was in it. Sergio didn't have a jack to change the tire, and the spare looked flat as well. We were in such a hurry to leave, we didn't take the time to check everything out the way we should have. Now we were stuck on the side of the road, in the middle of a desert, in the middle of the night. We didn't have any flares to alert the large tractor trailers, passing by at over 60 miles an hour. We began to pray for God to send us help, recognizing we had been a little foolish to take off without checking everything out first. It was very cold that night but we didn't know how to light the furnace in the trailer or turn it on. We could only wait for dawn for Sergio to walk to an exit for help. We made the bed up and all of us huddled together in it, putting on anything we could to cover us up. It was freezing. We turned the truck on several times and ran the heater from the engine, but it wasn't safe to leave it running, plus we would run out of gas. When the trucks would go by, it would shake the whole trailer. I realized how vulnerable we were just sitting on the curb of the road. My whole family could be wiped out if just one of those trucks hit us. I kept praying for God to protect us. I tried to sleep, but every truck that passed would wake me, plus I was so cold. The Lord finally spoke to me and asked me a question, "Do you trust Me?" Of course I trust you, was my response; "then go to sleep!" the Lord told me. I finally drifted off to sleep.

When the sun came up, Sergio got out to walk, but God sent a young couple who stopped and picked him up. They took him to the nearest exit and had the spare tire filled, then they brought him back and helped him jack up the trailer and change the tire. What a blessing! God had kept us through the night, and we learned two things: God can keep you through whatever danger exists, and always be prepared!

When we arrived in Los Angeles, the Aranda's took us to some apartments nearby where their sister-in-law, Maricela, lived. There was an open two bedroom apartment, so we took it. The Aranda's had a sofa in storage and a mattress they gave us. We shopped at a local thrift shop, and before long, we had our little home in LA. Our schedule was filled with preaching engagements all over the city. Doors had opened to preach in a church that was Korean, but had a Spanish congregation also. The pastors were a wonderful couple, Herman and Coni Sanchez, who had us come and minister several times. They knew a lot of pastors and so, new doors opened weekly.

While we were in L.A. one evening I was scheduled to preach, but a sharp pain hit my head. It soon developed into a major headache, like I had never had before. I could barely speak. It felt like "labor" in the brain. It was late in the afternoon, and I was laying in my darkened bedroom with a wet cold towel on my forehead. I had taken some pain medication, but nothing had helped. Sergio was concerned. Of course, he prayed for me, but as the afternoon progressed he was concerned I might need to see a doctor or something. I told him to just let me rest and pray for awhile. He was preparing to take my place at the evening

151

service when the Lord spoke to me and told me I needed to get up and go to the service, telling me "there was a soul involved". I told Sergio and he helped me to get up and get dressed. It was painful to even walk, not to mention the ride there. Every bump in the road felt like someone had hit me with a hammer in the head. When I arrived, I felt so weak, Sergio had to help me in. I sat down and stayed quietly in prayer as the worship service was in progress. Sergio explained when they announced me that I had been ill but God had told me to come, and then helped me to the microphone. My speech was slow at first, as it took every effort just to focus on the words. I brought the message the Lord had given me, and as I preached, I felt strengthened. People began to notice how it seemed as if I was being healed right before their eyes, because that was exactly what was happening! By the end of the message, the pain was completely gone! There was a young man there who was so touched that someone would make that sacrifice to bring the word of God, that he surrendered and came to the altar to give his life to Christ. There were several others who came to the Lord that night as well, and I went home totally healed! I learned early on how important obedience is and this was no different. God rewards those who will be obedient to Him.

We also were back on the air on HCCN TV in Los Angeles, as well as on the radio. Several Christian bookstores began to carry my book in their stores as well. In November, we had some services set up in San Francisco. We knew it would take a lot of prayer, going back into that area. There was always such spiritual resistance. The last time we were there, all the children were ill, and then the news of the death of Sergio's brother came. Still, God wanted us to go and share a message that He gave me for San Francisco. It was a warning to a city deep in sin and perversion that would suffer great consequences and judgment if they did not repent. God encouraged the believers to preach the truth with boldness and to not fear, for God would keep them in His hand. We packed for a short trip and left our little apartment for the services in San Francisco. We were not prepared for the trial that was ahead.

On the second week of our preaching in the San Francisco area, we received a call at our hotel room from Cuahtemoc. He had received a call from Lalo in El Paso. Lalo's wife, Maricela, had been killed in a car accident. She was crossing the street on her lunch break when a truck went through a red light and hit her, killing her instantly. We fell to our knees sobbing and began to pray. We tried several times to reach Lalo by phone, and finally that evening we were able to speak with them. The accident had occurred several days before, and they had her funeral and buried her. We could not find the words to express our grief. We asked if there was anything we could do, and he told us to just pray. Some friends had offered to take him and the children on a trip to Florida to spend some time away from home, away from it all. He thought it would be good for them to get away and spend time together to heal. They would be gone for awhile, so there was no point in our returning to El Paso. Our hearts ached for our dear friends. Christian was particularly impacted by it all, and very worried about Lily, but there was nothing we could do but pray. Two times we went up against the powers of darkness in San Francisco and both times tragedy struck. We were to learn that the Kingdom of God indeed suffers violence.

We spent Christmas in our Los Angeles home. This was the first time we had our "own" Christmas in a very long time, and after the losses of the past year, we welcomed some "alone" time. We bought a tree and some ornaments and put up some lights. It felt like a "normal" Christmas for once. It isn't easy living on the road, living out of a suitcase, and trying to raise a family while living with other families. I'm not complaining, as the blessings were huge, but sometimes you miss a "normal" life.

We received news that our dear brother Yiye Avila was coming to Los Angeles. He was holding a ministerial meeting with all of the area pastors at a auditorium in L.A. We were excited for a chance to see him again. A funny thing happened that night, when we arrived at the auditorium we ran into some of the evangelists from Yiye's ministry that were accompanying him. Yiye was back stage, so we told them we hoped we would get to see him some time after the service. I guess they must have told him we were there in the audience. There were several pastors who spoke prior to introducing Yiye. As irony would have it, I had to go to the bathroom. I didn't want to miss Yiye's message, so I got up and went while one of these men were speaking. While I was "out", they called Yiye to the pulpit and he preceded to announce that a dear friend and servant of the Lord was in the audience and asked sister Charlene Ramirez to stand. Sergio was sitting there, looking back to see if I had come back in the auditorium yet, but I was still washing my hands in the bathroom! Yiye looked out over the crowd and did not see me stand, but he did see Sergio, so he asked him to stand. Well, when I came back to my seat, Sergio whispered and told me that everyone in the room knew I was in the bathroom because Yiye had announced me, and I wasn't there to stand up. Boy, did I feel embarrassed! Oh well, these things happen to us all! Still, it was good to see him, and I was honored that he tried to present me to such a distinguished group of ministers from the southern California area. I'm sure the Lord chuckled at it!

We were all very happy to be "settled" again, but as the weeks went by, the service engagements began to decline, and we were running out of programs in El Paso. So we knew it was a matter of time until we had to pick up and hit the road again. We turned in the apartment and put our things in storage. We couldn't afford to pay for an apartment in LA while we were in El Paso. We had met a pastor from Santa Monica that had rental properties who told us when we returned he would rent us an apartment at a good price. The children were sad to leave LA, but since they had lived in El Paso and had friends there, they were happy to go and see them as well, especially to see Lalo and his family for the first time since the death of Maricela.

Our trailer home on wheels with Sharon in front

CHAPTER TWENTY
"On the road again"

We spent some time with Lalo and the family, but things had changed in many ways. He looked so thin, and there was a sadness in his eyes. The children had spent some time with some cousins in Mexico after they returned from Florida. We did not impose upon Lalo to coordinate for us this time. Instead, we just spent some time with him hoping to be of some kind of help. Lily remained very distant from Christian. He couldn't understand, but assumed it was because of the death of her mother. It broke his heart, as he wanted to be there for her, but she did not seem to want him around. I told him to be patient and let her grieve in her own way and time.

We had met another man in El Paso who asked if he could set up some preaching engagements for us. With Lalo going through so many things, we thought it might be a good idea not to burden him with setting up services for us, so we were happy the Lord had sent this brother to us.

One evening he asked us to accompany him to a pastors meeting in Las Cruces, New Mexico. It was very cold out that night, and we knew better then to take all the children to a pastors meeting, so Christian stayed at the hotel and babysat while we headed off to Las Cruces, (forty-five miles away.) We went in our trailer home, talking with brother Oscar all the way. Sergio somehow forgot to check the gas before we left. We made it there just fine, but on the way back home, he noticed the gas gauge was on empty. He decided to get off at the first exit to get gas, but we never made it that far. We ran out of gas in the middle of the desert. It was in the upper 20's, and he had left with just a suitcoat on. Sergio decided to take the gas can and try to walk to the nearest exit to get some gas, so I gave him my coat to help keep him warm. I wrapped myself in whatever I could find in the trailer, (which happened to be clothes from a dirty laundry bag.) Oscar and I stayed and prayed, but it was so cold, I had to put some dirty socks on my hands and feet to keep warm.

Sergio was kicking himself for not having checked the gas ahead of time. He was freezing, walking down a dark, cold, highway, dressed in a women's overcoat. As he walked along, he said every truck that passed by sent a rushing wind that went right through him. He was not in a good mood, to say the least, but then he felt the Lord was telling him to praise Him. Sergio began to sing a song to the Lord, and God began to fill him with joy. Before long, he said he felt like skipping; so he skipped along, swinging the gas can, praising God. A young man stopped and asked him if he needed a ride somewhere. He told him what had happened, so the young man told him to get in and he would take him to a gas station. He asked Sergio if he could ask him a question, and Sergio told him of course. He asked him, "What were you doing when I stopped to pick you up?" Sergio told him, "You may not believe this, but I was praising the Lord. It's easy to praise the Lord when things are going good, but when things are going bad, that's when it really counts." The young man stayed quiet, thinking about what he had just heard. When they exited at the next exit, (five miles down the road), he took the gas can from Sergio, got out, and filled the gas can. Then he got back in the car and drove him all the way back to the trailer. Sergio thanked him several times, and was about to get out, when the young man asked him to pray for him. He told him he was backslidden, and right there, he gave his life to Christ. God has a purpose for all the things we go through.

On top of all this going on, I was nearly frozen in the trailer, and Sergio had brought the wrong set of keys, so we didn't have the key to open the gas cap. Oscar got a rock from the side of the road, and they managed to "knock" the cap off. Still, we were all rejoicing because a sheep who was lost had come back to the fold. By the time we reached our hotel, my toes felt numb. I got in the shower and painfully and slowly, thawed them out. We were thankful God had sent us this young man or we might have frozen to death, but we were even more thankful to have lead him back to the Lord.

We had serveral wonderful services in El Paso. We went to some churches we had never been at before, including some services from the pastors in Las Cruces, before we began our trip back eastward.

After reaching Florida, we visited the church in Homestead. It was amazing to see the building God had provided them after Andrew. We heard all their wonderful testimonies and saw with our own eyes the rubble that was still in piles throughout the area. These brothers had learned first hand the blessings of being obedient in prayer and in serving the Lord with your whole heart. None of them suffered the damage that others had. It was great to hear their reports by mail, but even greater to witness it with our own eyes.

We were scheduled to fly out of Miami. We had called ahead to make sure the airline would accept our personal check, which they said they would. But when we arrived to the ticket counter, they refused to accept our check. We prayed, we tried everything, but they wouldn't budge. We took the limit we could take out of the ATM, which was $300, but that wasn't enough to pay for all of our tickets. Only half of us could fly, and we did not want to separate from each other. After we had prayed repeatedly, we sensed that God had a higher purpose. The airline told us we could go down to another airline that had a flight within the hour, and perhaps they would accept a check. We ran down to the other ticket counter and told them our predicament. They didn't accept personal checks either, but the ticket agent was a Christian, so she made an exception.

We proceeded to the gate, which was on another concourse than our original plane was. When we went through security, we asked the female guard if she could check our case through manually and not pass it through the scanners, as we were concerned it would erase our audio tapes. She seemed very agitated and was not friendly at all. She opened the case and took one of the tapes out. The message was entitled "Those that will remain behind". She burst into tears and started to call on the Lord. We recognized God had touched her, as we had always prayed that God's blessing would pour out on the tapes and touch whoever came into contact with them. She proceeded to tell us that she used to serve the Lord, but she left the ways of God and was now in this place of "hell". We led her back to the Lord in prayer and gave her some tapes.

When we left to hurry to our plane, she thanked us and smiled. She called ahead to have them hold the plane, and we made it on board right as they were about to close the door. Had we stayed on the first flight, we would have gone through another security check place and never met this "lost sheep". When God throws you a curve ball, there's always a reason. Sometimes I think we "miss" these opportunities by getting angry or frustrated, rather than looking to the Lord in prayer to see the "bigger" picture. When God says "All things work together for good to them that are called", He means it!

We returned once again to Puerto Rico, to check on Sergio's dad, and to do some work in preparing the second book for publication. We preached around the island for several weeks, and then a door opened for Sergio to go and preach in the Dominican Republic. A pastor had called to ask if either of us could go to preach there. We prayed and felt the Lord wanted Sergio to go, and it was confirmed when he went to preach at a church who gave him a special offering, which was just the amount he needed for the airfare. He had an amazing trip. When he returned he told us all about it.

He was met at the airport by this pastor who took him to his humble home. Sergio had prayed that he would have a place to sleep where he could have some privacy to seek the Lord and prepare, and that he would at least have a fan so the mosquitoes would not keep him up all night. The pastor's home didn't seem to afford him this, but he was there! They went to a service in a home that evening in a more affluent area. It was the home of a Christian man who had joined the church. He wanted to have a home meeting and invite his neighbors. The Lord moved greatly in the service, and at the end of the meeting, the brother asked Sergio to stay in his home. The pastor encouraged him to do so, and brought his suitcase from the car. This brother put Sergio in a private room which was air conditioned! God answered prayer!

Each day he preached in different places, including a radio program. At the end of the program, these women came to ask him to pray for their niece. She was a young girl that was dressed in a mini-skirt and seemed to have no interest in the things of the Lord. Sergio spoke with her, but she was very resistant. The aunts told him she once served the Lord, even sang at church, but she had turned to the world. They wanted her to return to the Lord, but the young girl was NOT interested. He tried to explain to these well meaning aunts that you can't force someone to make a decision to serve God, it has to come from their own heart. They left sad, disappointed that God had not touched their niece and returned her to the faith.

A few days later they received a call to go and pray for a baby that was very ill. They went to a small home and entered to find a young woman with a baby limp in her arms. Sergio laid his hands on her to pray, and noticed the child was burning with fever. He told all the people in the room to join in prayer with him. As they prayed, he felt the child's temperature go down. Then the toddler opened his eyes

160

and began to struggle to get down to play. The house had no doors in it, rather, the room was divided with curtains. From behind the curtain, a teenage girl came out in tears, and ran to check the baby. It was the same girl that the aunts had taken to the radio station! This was her sister's baby! Upon seeing the Lord heal the child, this young girl said she wanted to return to the Lord, and prayed with Sergio. The whole house rejoiced!

Another thing happened while he was in the Dominican Republic, he had mentioned the testimony of us running out of gas in the desert and how the Lord had used it to bring a man back to the Lord. Afterwards, on the way to minister with this pastor, the car broke down. They were far out of town and there was nothing around but a factory of some sorts that had a large fenced gate around it. The pastor tried to get the car to start to no avail. He told Sergio he was going to try to go and get some help. The pastor took off towards the factory. Sergio said about a half an hour later the pastor returned, closed the hood, and got in and tried to start the car. It started right up! Sergio supposed that perhaps the car was flooded with gasoline and he just needed to let it sit awhile, but the pastor told him, no, that was not it. The car was not going to start period, so as he walked for help. Then he remembered the testimony of what happened to us in the desert. He decided that there had to be a soul out there that needed the Lord. The only place he saw was the factory, so he approached the gate. There was a security guard there, so he began to talk with him. He said when the guard gave his life to Christ, he knew that when he returned back to the car it would start, and it did! Sergio shared this, and many other wonderful testimonies with us upon his return to Puerto Rico.

Around that time my father-in-law was turning eighty, so we had a special party for him. He was delighted because all of his grandchildren were present, which was a rare occurrence. He was such a wonderful man. He loved his grandchildren, and his chicken. He always was surrounded by chickens. He also loved sports, especially baseball. He had been a sports reporter, and played in the minor leagues when he was young. He and Christian spent hours of time watching ball games. The children loved him! It would be hard to leave him there all alone again. We tried to convince him to go with us, but he wasn't willing to leave. We knew he wanted us there, but God was calling us back to the ministry in the states. He understood, but still it was sad for all of us.

The "religious wars" were in full swing once again in Puerto Rico. God had me speak a warning to the island once again when we preached at Yiye Avila's ministry and then God told me it was time to leave the island. I was to shake the "dust" off of my feet and leave. It was a hard day, as we boarded the plane to the states and I did as the Lord had instructed me. I didn't know then that it was the last time I would go to Puerto Rico.

Preaching at the retreat in New York

CHAPTER TWENTY ONE
"A Focus in the West"

Our ministry became more focused in Texas and California. It is amazing how God had spoken this word to us and to see it come to pass. Doors opened more and more to us in Texas as well as New Mexico, Arizona, California, and Mexico. We traveled back and forth over the next few years.

On one trip, when we were about a hundred miles east of San Antonio, the camper started acting funny. It began sputtering and seemed to lose power. We were "crawling" along the interstate, in the middle of nowhere. We had services planned in San Antonio, and friends who would receive us, but we had to get there first. We prayed, but the sputtering not only continued, it seemed we were going slower and slower. I had little Benny sitting on my lap, and he spoke up and said, "Sing power, power, power". Sergio and I looked at each other, as we had been praying and praying, and nothing seemed to help, so we started singing "Power in the Blood" (the song Benny was referring to). To our amazement, the sputtering stopped and the camper picked up speed. Within minutes after we had stopped singing, the camper started losing power and sputtering again. Again, Benny told us to sing "power, power, power". So we sang it again, and immediately the camper stopped sputtering and picked up speed. We just looked at Benny, who was smiling, and commented it must be the Spirit of God directing us through our little boy. As long as we sang, the camper ran smoothly, and when we stopped, the sputtering returned, so we sang with Benny all the way to San Antonio! Out of the mouths of babes! God wanted us to know it was a spiritual battle and that we needed to stand firm in the power of the Lord.

We had new doors open in Phoenix, and opportunities to preach on the radio there. We also traveled down to Nogales and preached on both sides of the border. The list of churches we visited on these trips grew and it began to take us longer and longer to cross the country because of so many stops on the way. We rejoiced over all the new things God was doing in our ministry.

On one of our many trips back and forth across the country we had an experience that we will never forget. We had several services scheduled in Chicago, and upon arriving and heading towards a hotel, we were in a car accident. The interstate was under construction, and huge chunks were being cut out every fifty feet or so on the shoulder. It was bumper to bumper traffic, but at one point, it started moving a little faster, so we had picked up a little speed, when a car suddenly cut in front of us and then hit the brakes. Sergio swerved to miss him, entering us into the "shoulder" lane. He hit the brakes, but I could see one of the three feet deep "holes" a few feet in front of us, and knew we would not stop in time. I had laid Joshua (who had fallen asleep) down on the floor right behind the front seats, and over top of us, David was asleep. I yelled for the children to brace themselves and reached to grab Joshua, fearing David would fall down on top of him. Christian and Sharon were in the back with Benny, but before anyone could grab on to anything, we hit the hole. We fell in the hole with a tremendous impact, and partially "bounced" out of it. The impact was so hard, it knocked the toilet tank right off of the trailer, and bent the back axle. The cupboards had opened and books and things flew everywhere, yet none of the children were hurt. We all stepped out of the camper a bit dazed at what had just happened. Some people stopped to see if we were alright, having seen the whole thing happen.

164

Someone called the police on their cellphone. We were checking over each of the children to make sure none of them had been injured, when the officer arrived.

He began to chastise us for following so close to another vehicle. I tried to explain the car in front of us had just cut in front of us, we were not "tail-gating". Sergio came out of the "daze" and told the officer, "Excuse me, sir, but we need to pray." Right there, on the side of the road in Chicago, we all held hands and began to thank God and praise Him for keeping us through it all. When we finished praying, we noticed the officer had his head bowed in respect as well. His demeanor changed immediately, as he said, "You're Christians". He asked what he could do to help us. He had a tow truck come and tow our trailer to the hotel, and he put me and the children in his patrol car and took us there. He was originally from Puerto Rico, and he told me as a youth, he was part of a church, where he played in the praise and worship group. I asked him if he belonged to a church in Chicago, but he responded he had "gotten away from it". On the drive to the hotel, I was able to minister to him! We thanked him for his help and gave him books and tapes from our ministry, departing from him with the admonition to turn back to the Lord and to look for a church to go to. He recognized it was not a coincidence and asked us to keep him in prayer. God moves in such mysterious ways!

As it turns out, we had an auto club that not only picked up our hotel bill (due to the accident) but covered all our meals as well. The pastor of the church where we had a crusade had a member of his church who had his own auto shop. They thought at first the axle was not repairable, but this brother managed to fix it, and he only charged us for the parts. The church took up an offering to help us and it covered the full amount of the parts and then some. I truly believe all of this was for the purpose of God reaching that police officer. We had seen in the past how God uses trials and adversity to accomplish Spiritual goals.

We were getting used to having supernatural events happen in our life, as well as the many trials a life of faith involves. The second time we rented an apartment in Los Angeles we stayed there several months preaching in the area. We were sleeping one night while we were there, and were awaken to the entire apartment shaking violently. Pastor Aranda's son was spending the night with us, and he jumped up and stood in the doorway shouting, "EARTHQUAKE!" We were sleeping on a mattress on the floor, so I just sat there and praised the Lord as the whole room shook, and the windows rattled. Sergio tried to get up and walk, but the shaking was too hard to be able to walk without holding on to something. Christian, David and Sharon woke up a bit alarmed, but Benny and Joshua slept through it. It only lasted for about a minute and a half but it seemed much longer. We thanked the Lord for keeping us, and stepped out on the balcony to see what was going on. Car alarms were going off all over from the shaking. Our balcony faced the south, and as we looked out, we could see transformers exploding and lights going off further and further away, like watching a wave. We determined the epicenter had to be north of us, as this "wave" was headed southward. We thought it was somewhere near us, but in fact, the epicenter was in Northridge, about forty miles north of us. As many remember, freeway overpasses fell, and an entire apartment complex in Northridge collapsed down on itself. Several people died there. The amazing thing is that the churches in L.A. didn't suffer damage. In fact, they mobilized to help those who were homeless. People were sleeping in the parks as the aftershocks had them too afraid to go back into buildings. It was an opportunity for the church to minister to lives, and people came to Christ in the midst of this turmoil.

We returned to San Francisco, after a great deal of prayer and preparation (remembering our previous trips). This time was different, although there was oppression, there was also great blessing. We were in a service preaching, when a couple came to us and handed us some keys. We had mentioned how difficult it was to get around the city in the camper, and how difficult it had been to climb the hills of San

Francisco, especially the steep hill that led to their church. These people gave us their station wagon! They said they had planned to give it away to someone, as they no longer needed it, and when they heard us joking about how we barely made it there because of the "climb", they felt we were the ones they were to give it to. We were delighted, as it made it so much easier to get around in large cities like Los Angeles, San Francisco and New York. We also often had services for each of us to preach, but it was difficult to get to both with only one car. We praised God for this great blessing, as it meant we would be able to do much more than before.

Summer was quickly approaching and we had been invited to join with the church from Elizabeth, NJ, to go to their retreat. Sergi, (Sergito) Sergio's son, had joined us in Los Angeles, and was returning to Puerto Rico to be married in June. Thank God we now had two vehicles! We returned to El Paso, and while we were there, we met with our friend and coordinator Lalo and his family. Several years had gone by but the issue of Christian's feelings for his daughter Lily were still there. She had stopped showing interest in him after the death of his mother, but I think he never gave up hope. I told him if it was meant to be, God would change things. This time when we got together with them, we noticed Lily's attitude was different. She seemed generally friendly and interested in renewing her friendship with Christian. He was hesitant and uncertain what this meant, as he had begun to date another girl in Los Angeles, still he couldn't hide his feelings for Lily. He decided he would go to the retreat and seek the will of God. We drove both vehicles back all the way to Louisiana where Sergio flew with Sergi to Puerto Rico for the wedding, and the children and I continued on to New Jersey. (We didn't have the money for all of us to fly back). It was strange driving so far without Sergio at the wheel. Christian was a great help to me, he kept me company and took care of his younger siblings. Two weeks later, Sergio arrived with Sergi and his new bride, and we all went to the retreat together.

It was a great time in the Lord, a time of refreshing. Days were spent with teachings and visiting. There were about 200 people that were there. Many had trailer homes, others stayed in tents. The retreat was about 20 miles north of Binghamton, NY, way out in the country. The church owned the property, and they had bathroom facilities, but other than that, it was camping out. We would spend the day ministering, visiting different tents, sharing meals and there were games for the children. I imagine it was what the children of Israel experienced in the wilderness, however, this was no desert. It was filled with trees, and a creek where they would hold baptism services. At night, everyone would gather for the evening worship service and message. They would dance before the Lord for almost two hours before the message. It was a great time of rejoicing for all of us. The children and the adults would dance and join arms and go around in a large circle. There was such a unity and joy among the people. It was how I imagined God wanted His children to celebrate Him. God gave us tremendous messages to share. The Lord would often speak prophetically to the group, and His presence was so evident in the midst of us. What an experience! Christian, in particular, had an encounter with the Lord. I saw him dancing before the Lord with tears streaming down his face. I knew what was in his heart; he wanted to serve the Lord more than anything and he needed God's guidance. I prayed for the Lord to speak to him and reveal His will for my son's life. God spoke to my heart and told me that Lily was the wife God had for Christian, but told me I was not to say anything for the moment. When the retreat was over Christian wrote a letter to his girlfriend in Los Angeles and ended the relationship.

God provided Christian a car through a brother we met at the retreat. He was so excited to have his first car. Now that we had Sergi and his wife with us, it sure came in handy. We hit the road, with Christian, Sergi, Vanessa and David leaving ahead of us in their new car. We stopped in Louisiana to pick up our camper and headed westward. Christian had gone ahead with Sergi and Vanessa, as he was in a hurry to get back to speak with Lily. When we arrived, Christian and Lily had shared what God had been showing them both. I was at Lalo's house when they approached me to tell me God had revealed to them both that they were to be together but they wanted Him to confirm it. Lily told me the Lord told her to come and ask me, as He had given me the confirmation. I smiled and felt the Lord lead me to tell them what He had told me in the retreat. From that point on, we knew they would be married. Christian was not yet eighteen, but he had always been such a mature, serious young man, and a servant of God. I knew it would be a very special person who would be by his side in the ministry God called him to. We were delighted, but Lalo was not at first. He was concerned over them being so young, and so they agreed to wait until Christian was at least eighteen. Sergi and Vanessa were expecting a child and some complications arose so they stayed in El Paso and then decided to return to Puerto Rico. We left our camper with some friends in El Paso and continued on with the station wagon and Christian to Los Angeles. He had passed his GED and was going to be attending Bible College in Los Angeles. It was a hard thing for him to leave Lily, but he was headed to prepare himself for the future and the ministry that God had for them.

CHAPTER TWENTY TWO
"The LA days"

This time we rented another apartment in Bell Gardens. We would stay in this one for the longest time. A new ministry began to develop. I began to minister to groups of women at women's retreats, and noticed the great need many of the women of God had. The Lord began giving me messages and materials specifically designed for women. From this a group was formed, "Brides of Christ". We invited women from all the churches to participate in these retreats. We began to meet on a monthly basis as well. My dear friends, Herman and Coni Sanchez became very active and supportive in this new outreach, which we held in their church. Soon, more women wanted to come, but the distance for many to travel was quite substantial, so we formed three chapters, one in North Hollywood, one in Los Angeles, and one in Bell Gardens. It was amazing to see so many women with low self esteem issues, or that had been abused as young girls. Even pastors wives would come to be ministered to. It was a great time of God delivering many of His daughters from things that had held them back for years.

Doors continued to open all over. We visited churches all over Southern California and the San Francisco area. Doors even opened in Denver. We participated in a march for Christ in downtown Denver, with the church which invited us, and were invited to participate in a Christian TV program while we were there also.

Christian had enrolled in Bible College and got a job working at a bank. David and Sharon were enrolled in middle school. Los Angeles was home. When Christian turned eighteen he took a flight and went to see Lily with a ring in hand. She accepted his proposal and then several months later, she flew to see him. They planned a wedding for April. Lily and I went shopping in Los Angeles for material to make bridesmaid dresses. We had such a great time. While she was there I asked her to give her testimony at one of our women's retreats. I told all of the women to bring their daughters with them, and Lily shared about the death of her mother and how the Lord sustained her. She related that the last morning she had with her mother before she left for school, was a great moment when they were talking about dreams and the future, and telling each other that they loved each other. She thanked God for letting her have that last special memory with her mother. Then she told these young girls how you never know the last moment you may have with your mom, and not to let the last thing be a fight or harsh words, and to never miss the opportunity to tell your mother you love her. The altars filled with girls crying and hugging their moms. It was such a touching moment, especially when she told everyone that God had blessed her now with a second mother, and she hugged me. How blessed I was to have this wonderful young woman marrying my son!

When April came, Lily returned to Los Angeles to marry Christian. It was a very special day for us all. He was my first child to marry. I don't know how I made it through it without breaking down completely, but I managed through it all with quiet tears of joy. They found an apartment in LA and started their new life together.

Christian did very well at his job, but had some extraordinary events unfold. He actually went through two bank robberies while he worked there. In the first one, the thief had a shotgun which he aimed at Christian, ordering him to give him all his big bills. Christian gave him what big bills he had, but there were not many. The robber became irate and threatened to kill him if he didn't give him more. Christian told him that was all he had, so the thief went down the teller line, telling him he would shoot him when he came back if he didn't get him more money. Christian said he knew the Lord was with him. When the thief came back to him, he told him he had given him all he had, and the man decided after a few rantings, to leave and not shoot him. When he left, everyone was in shock. Christian, however, remained calm. The FBI came and was also amazed at how calm he remained and was able to recall descriptions and details. His bank was impressed with his behavior and promoted him.

The second robbery was after they were married. In this incident shots were fired and bullets flew everywhere. Christian had just entered for work and was in the back clocking in when he heard the gun fire. He dashed into the bathroom that was next to the time clock and stayed there until the shooting stopped. Then he exited, not knowing if the robbers were still inside or not, but he felt the Lord was telling him he needed to go and minister to others. There was one customer dead on the floor, and all of the tellers were hiding under the counters crying. The manager had him take them upstairs to the lounge to calm them down. It turned out that the customer that was shot was actually an accomplice, and no one else was harmed. The security guard had opened fire, and a gunfight ensued but the gunman got away. I was with Lily when we talked with Christian. He asked to speak to me about something, and then told me to remain calm. He asked us not to turn on the television, as it was all over the news. He told me briefly what had happened but asked me to keep Lily from seeing it until he could get home and explain to her. I was very alarmed as well, but managed to keep calm and not tell her, until he got home. Once again, his cool calm in the face of danger merited him another promotion, and now he was second to the manager at only nineteen!

Sharon always had a thing for animals. She and her friends had heard some kittens meowing, and found these kittens in the trash can, so before long, we had a kitten. Then there was the neighbor who didn't want to keep his rabbit any longer, so he gave it to her. On top of that, there was a pet store near our house, and she took some of her own money and bought a hamster, then another, and before long we had babies.

One day, she showed up with a fine looking dog, whom she claimed followed her home. He was a spaniel breed, and very well behaved. We put up flyers in the local stores to see if anyone had lost him, and kept checking the newspaper. This dog was beautiful as well as very well educated. We could see he was an expensive dog that someone had gone to a lot of trouble to train and groom. He had a gash in his upper shoulder near the neck, which looked as if someone had cut him open there. We tried to give him a name, but he didn't seem to respond to any of our names, until someone said "Buddy", to which he jumped and wagged his tail, so he pretty much picked out his own name. One day some men showed up claiming it was their dog. Buddy's reaction was obvious; he growled and all the hair stood up on his back. Sergio asked them what the name of the dog was, to which they replied "Colorino". Sergio told them to call him then, but the dog just hid behind us growling. We surmised that these men had taken the dog thinking they could sell him, and cut his ID chip out. He sure didn't want to go with them! Sergio told them the dog didn't seem to respond to them, to which they said it was actually their aunt's dog, and she had just given him to them. So he told them to come back with their aunt. They never did return, and Buddy became a valued member of the family.

While we were in Los Angeles, I received a call, that I was not expecting. I had seen my parents months before while we were preaching in Florida. We spent some time with them at a beach house. Daddy was doing well, although he was older, but it seemed he had completely recovered from a stroke he had a few years before. We had prayed with him them, and God restored him completely. Mother had her health issues, but she was doing well also. It was October of 1995. Sharon would soon have her thirteenth birthday. She had gotten involved with the Aranda's church youth group dance team. They performed in many different churches, even at a half time show in Los Angeles. We were looking forward to taking her and some of her friends to Magic Mountain for her birthday, but then the phone rang. It was my mother calling to tell me my father had passed away. I stood there with my heart pounding, not able to believe the words I had just heard. I asked her what happened. She told me she had taken daddy for a doctor's checkup that morning and he seemed fine. He had a little cold, and that was about it. She took him home and fixed him lunch, then she went to the pharmacy to refill one of his medications. She was gone less than an hour, and when she returned home, she found him on the floor. She called 911 and they were there in minutes, but they told her he was already gone. He had a massive heart attack, they believe, and died before he hit the ground. It was a shock to us all.

We went over all the options, should we all drive across country to be there, but that would take too long. We didn't have enough money for us to all fly there. Sergio knew my mother would need some time with me and my sister to sort things out, and then there was all the commitments we had in L.A. So it was decided that I would fly the next day and Sergio would stay in L.A. with the children. I had a peace in my heart as I knew my dad had given his life to the Lord. He had gone through so many health issues and operations over the years, that he asked me one time to pray that he would never have to go through that anymore, when it was his time that God would just take him, and I agreed and prayed with him. God had answered my prayer. He never suffered, and never returned to the hospital. My mother was comforted by this as well, still, it was a shock to us all.

I had the privilege to speak at his memorial service. It was a private memorial with just family present, as my father requested to be cremated. It took the grace and strength of the Lord for me to be able to speak and pay tribute to my dad, but God was with me. It was one of the hardest things I've ever done. I shared with the family how my father had given his life to the Lord several years before, as well as a vision the Lord had given me shortly after my dad passed away. I saw my father standing in a beautiful place. He was young, and he had both of his legs. He smiled at me and said, "Look kiddo, I got my legs back!" It was a comfort to all of us, especially to my mother.

I stayed on for a week longer to be with my mother, missing Sharon's birthday completely, but she understood. I called and talked with Sergio and the children every night, but I missed them so much, and I was still grieving about losing my dad. I knew he was with the Lord, but I missed him. I didn't have a chance to see him one last time. Still, I had no regrets, as I had always told him how much I loved him, every time we talked on the phone. I remember sitting with my mother a few days after the memorial service and talking about dad. I told her how sorry I always was about some of the mistakes I made when I was a teenager, and how I knew I let them down back then. I asked her if dad was proud of me and what I had done with my life. (No matter how old we get, we still have a need for our parents approval.) It was such a comfort to me to hear her tell me things that my father had told people, how he was so proud of his "baby girl" and all the things she had done for others.

My mother could see how much I missed my family. She felt the children needed me, so she told me to go back home. She assured me she would be fine. I left reluctantly, and yet relieved to be going home to my family.

At the Rose Parade in Pasadena
(left to right) Joshua, Charlene, David, Benjamin, Sergio and Sharon

CHAPTER TWENTY THREE
"The move back to El Paso"

As God had a way of doing things, when the preaching engagements in Los Angeles began to dwindle, doors opened more for us to return to El Paso. Christian and Lily had already returned to live there. The stress of Los Angeles and it's many dangers were too much. He had finished the Bible college course he had taken, and doors opened for them to return and work for the Lord in Juarez and El Paso. Now things were winding down for us as well in L.A. and the cost of living there was overwhelming. On one of our trips back and forth to tape programs in El Paso, the manager of the television station asked us if we would be willing to come and help at the station. As we prayed about it, we felt the Lord confirm it. On top of that, a pastor we knew was moving from a large house he had been renting at a very good price, and he offered us to take it over. All of the signs were pointing together, so we left our home in L.A. and traveled back to El Paso with all of our belongings in the camper, and all of the animals in the station wagon. We were all packed in like sardines!

Although El Paso is a large city, it seemed calm compared to life in Los Angeles. We enrolled all of the children in school. Benjamin and Joshua were now grade school age. Sergio and I began to help out at the television station. Before long the position as traffic director for programming was open, and the General Manager asked me to take the position. I had no previous computer experience, or television experience, except for being in front of the camera, but I felt led to take the job. I would pray, and God would direct me. I learned the computer programs and how to read grids and program guides. I even learned how to write FCC reports. In fact, I won an award from the TV Guide media for excellence in traffic management! They asked me how many years I had been a traffic manager, and I told them I had never done it before. I let them know God was the one who taught me what to do, and they STILL sent me the award. I still have the plaque.

Then one day the bookkeeper left the station, and so I helped out in accounting as well as in my job until they could hire someone else. I had previous bank experience from when I got out of high school, but this was all on computer. To top it all off, it was an old computer and one day it crashed! They had an expert come out to fix it, and he said he could not. We would have to invest in another system, but the station was a non-profit station, and there wasn't any money to buy a whole new computer system. I had learned that all things are possible with God, so I prayed over the computer and turned it on. I went to the system recovery (what I had seen the technician do, unsuccessfully) and prayed. God began to show me what to click, and before long, the whole system came back on line. The manager couldn't believe it and kept asking me how I did it. I told her I had no idea what I did, I just followed the Lord's leading. God restored our computer system! The technician couldn't believe it and kept asking me what I did, but the truth of the matter is I don't know what I did. I couldn't have repeated all the steps if I tried! They all knew I was a computer illiterate, so they knew it had to be God. There is nothing that the Lord can't handle! "Lean not to your own understanding, in all your ways acknowledge Him, and He shall direct your paths". Simple faith in God's Word trumps all, even modern technology!

The job took up a great deal of my time, but we still preached on the weekends. We went into Juarez a lot, as the need there was so great. Sergio was in charge of the phone counseling center at the station.

He had so many testimonies to share from this experience. One day a person called in who was about to commit suicide and he was led to the Lord. Many called in to ask for prayer for healing and received healing from the Lord. On several occasions we would take a week off and go to preach but now we would fly so as not to miss too much work. We preached in Providence, Rhode Island, we preached in Los Angeles, San Francisco, Jacksonville, and in Guadalajara, Mexico. On several occasions, Sergio would fly to see his dad for a few weeks, leaving me and the children in El Paso. This was the most settled we had been in a long time.

Christian and Lily had an apartment near us, awaiting the birth of my first grandchild! Only a few weeks before the birth, Lily's father called to tell her that her maternal grandmother was in the hospital in Juarez. Lily was in the process of applying for citizenship, and was not suppose to return to Juarez. Still, it would be the last chance for her to see her grandmother, as she was dying. Christian took her to Juarez to say goodbye to her grandmother. On the way back they were stopped at the border, and even though they explained the situation, Lily was detained. They spent the night at the border, but by daylight, all efforts failed, and they had to stay in Juarez. Lily had lost her right to return home to El Paso. She would have to stay in Mexico and file an appeal from there. Christian returned to work in El Paso, and to the apartment where they had just painted and fixed up the nursery. We tried making calls all day long, but there was no help. So Christian moved to Juarez to be with his wife. They rented a small place and a few weeks later, we got the call. We went to the hospital in Juarez to welcome Stephanie Joy. She was born on Sergio's birthday, and although he was Christians step-father, he said God had sent him Stephanie on his birthday, so that made him the official grandfather! It was a blessed time, as well as traumatic. It would be two years of waiting and living in Juarez, commuting back and forth to work for Christian, until he could finally bring his family home to El Paso. Through it all, they served the Lord and remained faithful.

Benjamin and Joshua were enrolled in elementary school, and really seemed to enjoy it. One day, when Joshua was in first grade, we received a call from the school that he had passed out in class and hit his head. We left the station and went to get him, taking him to the ER to be checked. It turned out that he had low blood sugar and passed out. Then he told us it was not the first time this had happened, but he didn't want us to worry. We learned not to let him go to long without eating.

David and Sharon were not doing as well in High School. While they liked it there, it was not a good influence in their lives. There were problems with gangs in the area, and many of these kids went to the local high school. We decided it was better to put them into a private Christian school. They also began going to an area youth outreach. A local church had rented a space behind a grocery store and they made an after school place for youth to hang out. On Sundays they would hold a youth service, with the purpose of evangelizing these youth. My children, David and Sharon, got very involved with this outreach. Still, there were a lot of kids from off the streets that hung out there during the week, and so some of the bad influences were still present.

We had many testimonies of miracles but none of them quite as astounding as one we witnessed in Juarez. God had given us a message to call the churches to a day of prayer. We announced it for several weeks over our television program, and on the radio. God gave us a specific day for us to join together across El Paso and Juarez to pray. There were several events planned in El Paso, but we went to an open air service in a park in Juarez. Several churches joined with us there. We had a platform and a sound system set up. Many people were at the park. We had a time of praise and worship followed by periods of prayer being led by different pastors. Sergio and I both spoke and shared why the Lord had called us to prayer, and prayed with the people as well. When the service was nearing the end, the Lord led Sergio to call the people forward who needed specific prayer. A lady came to us and asked if we could go to pray for her child who was sitting in the audience. She said he could not speak and the doctors were not able to help him. She told us he was able to make some grunting sounds but could not speak.

We went to pray for the young man, and after praying, Sergio asked him to say the name "Jesus". To our surprise, the young man smiled and said in a whisper, "Jesus". The mother let out a shout, and Sergio asked him to repeat it. He said "Jesus" even louder. The mother began to cry. Realizing that God had done a miracle, Sergio wanted everyone to be able to hear it, so he went up on the platform to get a microphone. The young man got up and followed him. The mother began to scream and jump up and down. She almost collapsed, and someone had to hold her up. The young man said "Jesus" three times over the microphone. The mother screamed out, "He couldn't walk either!" We were all amazed and began to praise the Lord. Seeing the miracle, God moved us to give an altar call for lives to come to Christ. This mother gave her life to Lord right then and there, as did many others. A local Juarez Christian publication was present and took pictures and reported on the miracle the Lord had done in response to the obedience of His people to come together in prayer. God had poured out his blessing because His people had humbled themselves in obedience and prayed.

While we were in El Paso, we met a lady pastor who invited us to preach at her church. After we had preached there several times, she asked us to stay on and help with teaching a discipleship course.

While working with this church, the Lord gave me a special word for the church, and so one Sunday evening, the pastor had me bring the word to the church. The Lord poured out His Spirit and moved mightily. For the following Sunday nights, I would preach, and God kept doing more and more marvels. It got to the point that there was standing room only. There was an elderly man who had been diagnosed with a serious heart problem. There was nothing that could be done except to have a heart transplant. He was very weak and needed oxygen, but he would still come to church. On one of the

Sunday nights, while we were praising the Lord, he began to dance! We all watched amazed as he seemed to gain more and more strength. He was weeping and praising the Lord as he danced around the room. He said he felt that the Lord had healed him. When he returned to the doctor, he was told they couldn't explain it, but his heart was as healthy as a fifteen year old! God was bringing revival to El Paso!

Then, as suddenly as it began, one evening the pastor announced it was the last night of the revival services. I was shocked! Why would you bring an end to such a move of His Spirit? It turns out a deacon went to the pastor with a tale of a dream she had where she said someone had come and taken over the church. Somehow the devil managed to fill the pastor with the fear she might loose her church to me. I told her I had no desire to start a church of my own, neither did Sergio. We were there to help churches grow and become stronger. We would never divide a church or seek to "steal" someone's sheep. This was not an issue of either of us "taking control", it was a move of the Spirit, and He could move through anyone who was willing to surrender to Him. The church was in shock as well. They were receiving such blessing, and couldn't understand why it should stop. The Word of God warns us not to "quench" the Spirit, neither "grieve" the Spirit, which indicates that our actions can be like a bucket of water thrown on a fire if we're not careful, and that's exactly what happened.

The church went down from there. When God decides to "visit" a church, and they become afraid of loosing "control", so they quench the Spirit, the blessing departs. It had been a special time for us as well, as we were receiving blessing from the Lord also, and it was a very sad experience. Neither of us could understand why this had happened, but we understood it was God who had been shut out, not us. Still, we respected the authority of the pastor and did not express our disappointment publicly. We were led at that point to leave and go to another church. This church dwindled down to only a few people, the pastor went through a divorce, and eventually the church closed.

It was sad for us to see what happens to those that don't appreciate a visitation from the Lord.

God began to move and use us in another congregation where we stayed for the next couple of years. We became good friends with the pastors there, Charles and Yolanda Wilson, and they became part of our weekly television program. They were very sensitive to the leading of the Spirit, and we had great times in the Lord with them. We had a lot of dear friends who were faithful viewers of our program and who helped maintain it on the air.

God would often give me prophetic messages that I would write and share over the air as well as send out to people with a monthly newsletter. Dimas would still translate them for me as he had through the years. By this time, we had two books published in Spanish, and we were quickly nearing enough to publish a third volumn. The first of these messages had been published in English as well, but we rarely had the opportunity to preach in English speaking churches.

Sergio seemed to be preaching more in Juarez. It was always a very moving experience to go to Juarez. The poverty level was impacting. With only a river separating Mexico from the United States, the drastic difference was ever evident. There were areas of Juarez that were no more than a one room brick building that housed families of eight or more. We often saw places that had no electricity or water. When the rains come in the desert, they come in torrents and often cause flash floods. There were a few of those that wiped out the little that some of these people had. Then there is the heat of the summer and the lack of clean water to drink, or the freezing cold of a winter night in the desert, where many died because of no heat. It is a very harsh existence. We would always find children and women, or handicapped people at all hours, begging in the streets. They would gather at the border crossings and go from car to car as the people were waiting in line to cross the border. The conditions were deplorable in many areas, while in other areas of Juarez, the affluent lived, oblivious to the plight of their own people. Many of the churches would send help over, and we would often take things over to give to the poor. Still, it often seemed just a drop in the bucket.

At Christmas time, the military base would gather toys for children, as well as the churches, and distribute to the poor. Most every border town was the same. People would travel north to the border, in the hopes of being able to cross to America. The waiting list to come in legally was years long. Many of them found themselves stranded and in poverty, with little hope of being able to afford the "fees" the "coyotes" charged to smuggle them across the border. Those that crossed by night illegally were often detained and deported. Many were used by drug lords to transport illegal substances. When you view the poverty level there, and can stand in plain sight of U.S. soil and see the blessings so close at hand, there's no wonder as to why people get desperate waiting and cross illegally. They have no hope where they are. They can't feed or provide for their families, and so they run the risk of being incarcerated if they are caught, just to have the opportunity to provide a better life for their children.

There was not alot we could do, but as Peter said, "silver and gold have I none, but what I have, I give you". We gave them the Word of God, and whatever else we had available to share. The gospel was growing in Juarez, as the station reached into Juarez with the Word, and churches began to appear all over the city. Where drugs and violence was overwhelming, the Lord had lifted up a standard. One night we preached in Juarez on a mountain top at a man's home. He had a few chairs sitting out, and had invited his neighbors. He had a small amplifier and microphone set up, and that night God did a big miracle.

When we arrived there, as the people were singing, I went to the side to pray. As I looked out at all the lights of the city below, the Lord spoke to me and told me there were lives in the city below that He would reach that night. I remember asking Him how that was possible, as the little amplifier could barely carry enough sound for those that were there. He told me to look out, and as I did, He told me He would cause the message to be heard, like an echo, flowing through the streets. Now, I already knew that nothing was too hard for the Lord, so I just believed if He said it, He could do it.

When it was time to bring the message, the Lord led me to share part of my testimony. At one point, I felt led to say, "I can't see you, but you can hear me. If you want to accept Jesus into your heart, just raise your hand right where you are, and pray this prayer with me." I continued on to pray the sinner's prayer, and lead "by faith" those people who I believed had heard, and were praying with me. When the service was over, a group of people arrived saying that they had heard our voices and recognized it was us, as they had heard us so often on TV. They thought someone had the TV up loud, and that we were on the air, but they could not find us on any station. They went outside and said they heard our voices echoing down the street, so they followed it until it led them up the mountain to where we were. We were amazed! God had done what He said He would do!

But the biggest testimony came the next day when a woman called us at the television station. She said she lived in Juarez and the night before she heard our voices in the street, but she couldn't see us anywhere. She said there was this group of young boys, gang members, that stopped and were listening to the message on the street corner across from her house. She said at one point she heard my voice say, "I can't see you, but you can hear me. If you want to accept Jesus into your heart, just raise your hand right where you are." She said to her amazement, these young boys raised their hands and followed the prayer, giving their lives to Jesus, right in front of her house! We received other calls inquiring if we had been in Juarez preaching the night before, as many said they could hear our voices in the street, all of them confirming what the Lord had done, but the testimony of the gang that gave their life to Christ was the greatest.

At work at KSCE-TV in El Paso, Texas

CHAPTER TWENTY FOUR
"The event which changed us all"

It was the summer of 1999. Sergio and I had been asked to go and preach at a ministers conference in Chicago. They provided our airfare and hotel, so we left on a Thursday and returned on Sunday evening. It was an interesting trip, but after arriving, we realized that this group of pastors had some different ideas than we did. It was a relatively new "denomination", which on the surface seemed very on fire for the Lord, but the leadership was more like a dictatorship. Still we preached what the Lord gave us to preach. The people seemed very blessed, but the leader didn't seem very happy with us. We had spoken about keeping your eyes on Jesus and not on men. We ministered on the dangers of "falling away" and being "deceived" when you follow doctrines of men instead of the Word of God. This is what the Lord led us to do, as we knew that the "truth" of the Word of God would set people free. We returned not knowing why God had sent us there for sure, but we never heard from this group again.

Then came Tuesday night, and Sharon arrived at home with her friends that evening and asked us if she could spend the night at one of their houses. My first reaction was to say no, but she insisted she would go straight there and would be on time at her summer job the next day. Her father thought it was fine, so I finally agreed. She was with her best friend, Jessie, whom we had seen come to the Lord, and had been at her baptism service just a few months before. The other girl, Amanda, was a good friend of David's, and seemed like a nice girl. They did as they said they would do, and went straight over to Amanda's house. What I did not know was that Amanda's mother was out of town and she was staying by herself in the house. Sharon was sixteen years old at the time.

Around two thirty in the morning, the phone rang. It was from a hospital telling us our daughter had been in an accident and they needed us to come to the hospital. Waking out of a sound sleep, I was a little disoriented, and tried to get them to tell me how she was, but they just asked for us to come, and to not speak with anybody, which I found rather strange. Still, as we dressed and left for the hospital, we prayed, and I felt a peace that God was with her. This song kept going through my mind, a Spanish song, which says, "and when you look at me, you fill my heart with peace." I remember telling Sergio that God was letting me know that He was with Sharon.

When we arrived at the hospital, which was the Army Medical hospital, (the closest to our home), there was a woman who was waiting in the parking area for us. She identified herself as being with the police department in "victim services". She led us into the hospital, telling us that there had been a serious accident and our daughters injuries were still undetermined. When we entered through emergency I could hear the screams of my Sharon. I wanted to go to her immediately, but they told me it was not possible, and led us to another room where there were some police officers waiting to speak with us. They began to ask us questions as to what color hair our daughter had, which seemed odd to me, as I could hear her screams. They told us she had been seriously injured and that a doctor would come in to explain the extent of her injuries. They explained that three girls had been in an accident which involved a roll-over, which they believed happened as a result of loss of control, because there were no other vehicles involved. We asked concerning the condition of the other girls, to which the officers got very quiet, and one of them looked down at the floor. It dawned on me, in that instant, and I cried out, "they're dead aren't they?", to which they nodded their heads. I remember going on my knees sobbing, and Sergio joined me as we prayed for the families of these girls and for our daughter. Shortly after, the doctor came in to inform us of our daughters condition.

She had broken both femurs (the thigh bones), and one had poked through her flesh. She lost part of a toe, dislocated her arm, and they weren't sure, but it seemed she did not have any internal injuries to any vital organs or to her spinal column. She had cuts and bruises, and a large gash in her leg where a section of her leg, about eighteen inches long, had been ripped away, down to the muscle. Our heads were reeling. I had thought they would say she broke an arm, or had a mild concussion, but this was more that we were prepared to hear! Still, as the reality dawned on us, we were grateful that she was alive, and praised God for keeping her in the midst of this. I asked if they could please give her something for the pain, but I was told that she had lost so much blood, that the only thing keeping her alive was adrenaline. They were still determining the extent of her injuries and once they stabilized her, they would give her some pain medication, and let us see her.

Sergio and I held each other. At one point, I thought he might pass out, then he excused himself and went to the bathroom. When he came out, his color was back and he told me he had gone on the floor in the bathroom before the Lord, and God had spoken to him. He told me the Lord told him to not be afraid, and to remember that our family was in covenant with Him. These words gave him strength and comfort, as they confirmed to me what the Lord had already placed in my heart, the Lord would save our daughter, and she would be well.

Some time after, the doctor returned and told us they would be taking Sharon to surgery shortly, but we could see her first. He led us to radiology, where they had taken her for x-rays, and we were finally able to see her. I was not prepared for what I would see. Our daughter was swollen up to the point she looked like she weighed over 300 pounds. Her eyes were blood red, and they had her legs covered with a sheet, which is probably good, or I think I would have passed out right there. She had blood and bits of glass all in her hair. She began to cry when she saw us and kept asking us to "forgive her". She was more worried about upsetting and hurting us than she was about herself. Of course, we held her hand and reassured her of our love. She was medicated and could say very little, but she did ask about her friends. We were told by the doctor to not tell her about the death of her friends, as she was "fighting" for her life, and was in no ways "out of the woods" yet. We told her that they had taken her friends to another hospital, and she didn't ask anything more. (They had taken them to another hospital, to the morgue).

We explained she would be going to surgery and began to pray with her. The x-ray technician was a Christian as well, so he joined us in prayer. It was a comfort to us that God had surrounded her with so many dedicated people. Her doctor promised us that he would do everything in his power to save our little girl, and was so kind and compassionate. He had a team of orthopedic surgeons that worked on her for over ten hours. While she was in surgery, we prayed and prayed. God showed me a vision of her lying on the table with a bright light surrounding her, and told me that it was His Holy Spirit hovering over her. When it was all over, this same doctor, who stayed through the whole ordeal, came to tell us it was nothing less than a miracle that she made it through the surgery without any complications whatsoever after all the trauma and blood she had lost. We knew God had been faithful.

She was in intensive care with a respirator, unable to speak to us, for the first few days. We stayed at her side, as long as we could. Often, tears would stream down her cheek, and she would try to say "Jessie" or "Amanda". We knew she was concerned for her friends, and we dreaded the day we would have to tell her they were gone. The doctors came to explain to us that there was still a great danger of her having an embolism, as the fat in the femur bone can enter the circulatory system and travel to either the heart or brain. There was a 25% chance of that happening with just one broken femur, but that increased to 75% with both femurs broken. They had her on blood thinners, but they could not offer us any guarantees. She would have to remain in intensive care on monitors for four days, and they did not want us to tell her any bad news until they were sure she was stable.

I remember holding her hand and praying, and telling her how Jesus had told us she would be alright, when the tears began to roll down her cheek again. Suddenly I knew she had an experience with Him. I asked her, "Did you see Jesus?", to which she nodded her head "yes", and I saw a smile. I could see she wanted to tell me, but she was unable to speak with the tube down her throat. I told her she would have plenty of time to tell us all about it soon. On the third day they took out the respirator tube, and though heavily medicated, she would have lucid moments when she would tell us more about what had happened that night.

They had gone to Amanda's house, as they had promised. Around midnight, Amanda wanted to go out and get something from the 7-11 store and take a drive. Sharon and Jessie didn't want to go, but then Sharon thought about how it wasn't safe for Amanda to go by herself, so they agreed to go along with her. After they stopped at the store, they took a drive on the outskirts of town. It was a hot night, and they were driving with the windows down, listening to music. Amanda began to play around with the music. They were in her grandmother's mini-van. She started to flash the lights on and off and "rock" the vehicle to the rhythm of the music. Sharon said she told her to stop, as they couldn't see where they were going, but Amanda continued to do it. At one point, she flashed the headlights on only to see that she had gone off the road. This was a big two lane highway that went out of town, out near where we lived. The speed limit is 55mph, and they were going around 60mph. Amanda was only sixteen and did not have the experience driving to know how to control a vehicle properly. When she saw she was off the road, she yanked the wheel, over compensating, and went off the other side of the highway. In an attempt to correct, she yanked the wheel in the other direction and tried to hit the brake, but missed and hit the accelerator, sending the van in a roll, which rolled the vehicle violently over and over, for 210 feet. Sharon said when she first saw they were off the road, she called out to God to save them, because she sensed it was going to be bad.

The van rolled into the desert and finally came to a rest. Sharon said it felt as if someone had thrown her in a barrel and thrown her over Niagara Falls. She said she had her eyes open, but she couldn't see anything, or feel anything. Then a light appeared, and the form of Jesus was before. He spoke to her through his eyes, into her spirit, telling her it was not her time. He had a purpose for her, and she was going to be alright. When He disappeared, her sight came back, as well as her feeling, and she could feel intense pain. She called out to her friends, but no one answered. She was sitting in the passenger seat originally, but now she found herself on the floor in between the two front seats. She saw a leg wrapped in the steering wheel, and another one was out through the windshield. She couldn't see into the back seat to see how Jessie was, but she could see Amanda in the drivers seat next to her. She seemed to be unconscious, with blood coming out of her ear.

Someone heard her scream and came to the van. It was a young couple who had seen some lights off the road in the desert, who stopped to check it out. The girl stayed with Sharon and the boy ran back to the highway and waved a passing tractor trailer down. The truck driver got on his radio and called for help. Within ten minutes an ambulance responded. They had just been on a call out in the neighborhood near the outskirts of town and got there quickly. All these things were God's hand on her. That road is very isolated and not well traveled at one in the morning. These were not coincidences, but God's mercy on her, on us all. The EMT's reviewed the situation, and at first thought they had three dead girls, until they heard Sharon scream. She was trapped inside a smashed mini-man, but they managed to get her out. She said when they moved her the pain was unbearable. They put some kind of "suit" on her and blew it up. Then they put her on a "board" and transported her to the ambulance. (What she didn't know was that Amanda's head had gone out the window on one of the rolls, smashing her skull, and the door had come off the mini-van and Jessie had been thrown in the air, landing on her head, snapping her neck. They were killed instantly.)

She found herself in the hospital being poked and prodded from every angle, in severe pain, begging them to get in touch with her parents. She said the next thing she remember after seeing us in the hospital was this peace that came over her as they wheeled her into the surgery area. She said there was this blinding light all around her. She asked the pre-op nurse if she could turn the light off, but the nurse told her there was no bright light on. She felt this warmth over her, like a blanket. (I told her how the Lord had shown me His Holy Spirit hovering over her). God kept her through the whole ordeal!

The news spread rapidly about the accident, and before long all of her friends were at the hospital. They held "watches" through those first four days when she was in intensive care. At times there were over twenty kids in the waiting room. They knew they couldn't go in and see her, but they just found comfort being there. Some of them brought us food, and cried with us. Some of these kids were the kids from the streets, who had been touched by our daughter and her story. They showed so much love and devotion, praying for her together. Some had painted hair, black fingernails, chains and black leather clothes, but the love and compassion they displayed was a lesson to us. While only a few Christian friends came, these kids stood watch and prayed for us all. I learned a lesson then and there that you can't judge a book by it's cover.

At the same time, David was going through the trauma of it all, as we all were, but he had lost two dear friends, as well as the trauma of his sister, who was one of his best friends. What we didn't know at first was that he felt guilty because they had asked him to go along earlier that night, and he said no. Somehow he blamed himself, thinking if he had been with them and had driven, it would have never happened. I could see how much he was hurting, but Sharon needed me to be there with her. Then there were Benny and Josh at home. How was I suppose to be there for everyone? Chris and Lily came over to take care of Benny and Josh, and Sergio went back and forth between the hospital and home. Christian came on the third night and insisted I go home to get some rest and he stayed with Sharon. Some of David's friends stayed with him, as they promised me they would, and helped him get through it.

On the fourth day, when they determined she was "out of the woods", they transferred her to a private room, so we could finally answer her questions about her friends. It was one of the hardest moments in our life. Sergio told her her friends had not made it. We had to listen to sobs of a broken heart, as we held her and comforted her. But God has a way of doing things. Here she was, a young girl, in terrible physical and emotional pain, with her legs so badly scarred and unable to walk, yet she thanked God continually for sparing her life. She told all her friends, the nurses, everyone, that she had seen the Lord, and what He had done for her. The peace and inner strength she displayed was awe inspiring. God sent a young medic that night to her room. When he entered the room they both just stood still and stared at each other for the longest time. Sergio and I looked at each other in amazement. In the midst of death and dispair, God had sent someone that sparked life and hope in her again. They formed an instant bond. He took such good care of her. They would talk and talk. Suddenly, she was alive again. When she had a particularly rough day, like some of the first days she started physical therapy, or when they had to do more tests, he would show up and cheer her up. His name was Andrew Harrold, but he told us to call him Alex.

Her arm had dislocated again, and had to be reset. She was in immense pain. I tried to help her through it by teaching her how to do some breathing techniques they teach you for childbirth. It seemed to help, but even with that and the pain medication, she screamed as they tried repeatedly to get her arm reset. I tried to be strong for her, but when it was all over, I went in the hall and cried. Alex came and put his arm around me and tried to comfort me. He was such a kind, compassionate young man. That evening he had her laughing and talking. He would often come in on his off hours just to spend time with her. I knew God had sent him to give her encouragement and some measure of joy in the midst of such a horrible experience.

About a week after the accident, they took off the bandages and Sharon saw her legs for the first time. We were worried how she would react as a sixteen year old girl, but as she looked down at all the scars and the large gash out of her leg, she looked up and smiled saying, "well, at least I've got legs, and I will be able to walk again!" She never complained or said "why me?" She found the way to thank God through it all. One afternoon as we talked, she told me she knew that Amanda would have been overwhelmed knowing she had been responsible, and Jessie would never have survived it if Sharon died, having come from a very traumatic childhood, so she understood why God took them and left her. She said, "I thank God that He chose me to suffer this for His Glory." I could hardly believe my ears. What an attitude from such a young girl! She told everyone about it, including a young man who had been in an accident who was very bitter. The nurses wheeled her down to his room, and she ministered to him! Her testimony became widely known in the hospital as well as in the community. We were so thankful to God, and so proud of her!

They performed a skin graft on her leg to try to cover the missing part of her leg. They said she would always have a section from the muscle and tissue that was missing, but they would try to graft skin from her thigh over the wound area. They told us it would take several grafts, but the first skin graft took 97%, and she never had a need of more grafts. (I was told later by a scientist who works in skin graft technology that this in itself was a huge miracle, as they have never been able to obtain that level of results. The best they could achieve in lab controlled experiments was a 45% success.)

On the 21st day after the accident, she was discharged and allowed to come home. It was our twentieth anniversary. What a gift the Lord gave us! We had a hospital bed put in the living room and began the home recovery part of her restoration. She was not able to stand at first, but within weeks she began to feel stronger, and as she went to therapy, she began to take the first steps, and then to walk. They had not been sure if she would need further surgeries, and if the bones would match. One of the femurs had broken with a piece lodged up in her upper thigh. There was no way of knowing for sure if they would be equally measured, or if they would need further proceedures for her to be able to walk without a severe limp, but none of that was ever a concern, as she walked perfectly normal. What they expected to take months of therapy happened in weeks. No one could explain how her bones were mending so quickly and so perfectly, but we knew it was the Lord.

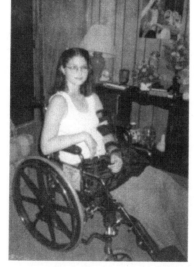

Sharon 6 weeks after her accident

195

CHAPTER TWENTY FIVE
"Life goes on"

Why do certain things happen? I can't answer that question. All I know is that the Lord said in His Word, "All things work together for good", so we always realized there was a purpose, and so did she. Shortly after the ordeal, she told me a dream she had a year before the accident.

In the dream, she was taken to heaven, where everyone was dressed in Army uniforms. She said it was like a boot camp. This one angel was like a drill sergeant. She said everyone she met there seemed to know who she was, and they told her God had a purpose in her life and that one day He would take her to this place. In the dream she saw a demonic creature that paralyzed his victims with fear. This angel showed her how to defeat this creature by looking into its eyes with the "light of truth". Oddly enough, she dismissed it as just a dream until she woke up from surgery in an Army hospital where everyone was dressed in uniform. She remembered the dream, and how she was taught how to defeat the demon of fear. When she felt overwhelmed, attacked by fear and pain, she held fast to the truth the Lord had given her that night, God had a purpose for her life and she would be alright.

When you go through an event such as this, it takes time to process it all. We will be eternally grateful that God saved our baby girl. We recognize His blessing in our life, and can only praise Him more and more for His mercy and faithfulness. But to say that this event hadn't changed us, would be untrue. It changed us all. We began to look at things as "before the accident" and "after the accident", as if our lives had been divided by some strange cosmic event. To say we were aware, or grateful of God's blessing before this, would be true, but not in the way that we were after the event. Even the small things that people take for granted became motives of great praise and rejoicing. I remember going by her room one day. She was laying across the bed on her stomach, reading a book, with her legs swinging in the air. It brought me to tears. I went and got Sergio, and we just stood there in the doorway, her oblivious to our presence there, and tears filled our eyes.

On another occasion, our car broke down, we had little money, one thing after another, and Sergio was very frustrated. I took him to her room, and as we looked in at her sitting there listening to music, I told pointed to her and told him, "she's alive!" Immediately, he began to thank God and stopped fuming about the little trials we were going through. It changes the way you look at things. Gratitude is not a big enough word to describe how we feel as parents.

I can't say we didn't have any negative moments. I went through a very dark time about six months after the accident. I began to having bouts of depression. Some of the old things that had tormented me so many years before seemed to be hovering around again. I think it was partly due to the fact that I questioned my responsibility involving the accident. I was the last parent that spoke to the girls before that event. I began to blame myself, thinking if I had done differently, perhaps the girls would still be alive. I know it was the enemy attacking me, but between that and the change of life, it was a hard time. I tried to stay in the Word and drown the negative thoughts out.

Then Sergio's father became ill and he had to fly to Puerto Rico to take care of him. He was gone for a month. I didn't have my best friend there, the one person who had a way of always making me smile. On top of that, I would pray but it seemed if God was not around either. My knowledge of the Word told me this was far from the truth, but my emotions were all over the place. I felt guilty feeling sad after God had saved my daughter from death, so I would repent and ask God to please forgive me for feeling sorry for myself. The spiral of depression kept bringing me down. No one knew. I was very good at "keeping up". I needed to be strong for everyone else. Sergio would call every few days, and I knew he was going through a hard time taking care of his dad, and he missed us all, so I didn't want to bring him down.

One day he felt led of the Lord to pray for me, and he called me later to see if I was alright. I broke down and told him some of what I was going through. We prayed together over the phone. That night as I layed in bed, God spoke to me and reminded me of the time Jesus was in a boat in the middle of the storm, and had fallen asleep. His disciples went and woke him, asking him if he didn't care that they were going to perish. Jesus rebuked them for their lack of faith. I wondered why He was telling me this. He asked me if I knew why He rebuked them, afterall, they came to Him believing He could fix it, didn't they? I thought about it for a moment and then began to wonder, why did he rebuke them? They obviously believed if they woke Him up, He could do something, so it seems they did have some faith in Him. God explained to me, like them, I believed HE could do something, but I didn't believe I could do something. Hadn't God told them they could do the things that He did? They believed in Him, but they didn't believe what He said about them. He told me, "You believe I can do it, but you don't believe YOU can do it." It was as if a light went on. I suddenly understood why my prayers did not seem to be getting anywhere. I kept asking God to do it for me, and God was waiting for me to believe His Word and take the authority He gave me to do something about it. Sometimes we feel helpless, but God has made us more than conquerors. You can't conquer anything if you don't believe you can. When Sergio called back I told him what the Lord had showed me and how His truth had set me free.

When Sergio returned home, I was the same old Charlene again. However, within weeks we received news that his father, (who had gotten better while he was there), had passed away. Once again, Sergio would have to make the trip back to Puerto Rico. We all wanted to go, but there was no money for us to make the trip with him. I had planned a special surprise birthday party for him for his fiftieth birthday, but then the news of his father came. I told him of the party we had planned, as under the circumstances, I wasn't sure it was the right time to "surprise" him. At first, he wanted to cancel it, then he thought about it and told me perhaps it would be better to be with family and friends. So the party turned more into a comforting memorial to his dad, which gave us an opportunity to grieve together the day before he left for Puerto Rico to bury him. Sadly, we put him on the plane. I wanted so much to be there for him, but he felt I needed to be with the children. He knew his father had come to the Lord and was ready to go be with Him. His dad was not at all happy watching himself deteriorate, so Sergio was at peace, especially when they told him that he did not suffer. Still, I was sorry I could not be there for him.

The accident caused Sharon to grow up before her time. She said she couldn't go back to school, as she felt so out of place there. Suddenly, the things of teenage girls seemed small and trivial to her. She finished school at home and got her GED, then decided to go to community college. In the midst of it all, she met a young soldier from Pennsylvania, Jonathan McCoy, and before long he asked her to marry him. We didn't want to have her grow up so fast, or move away, she had barely turned eighteen. Perhaps we should have put our foot down and made them wait, but honestly, we knew she would just run off with him. She had come so close to death, and now she was living at full speed. We had watched her suffer so much, and we almost lost her. I couldn't bear the thought of losing her. She seemed happy, and at that point, I just wanted to see her happy. She had suffered enough loss in her young life.

Life went on in El Paso, but we no longer worked at the Television station. I had quit to take care of Sharon. We traveled preaching once again, but this time with just Ben and Josh. David and Sharon were in college. Soon Christian and Lily gave us another grandchild, Katie Grace. They were leading a home group through their church, and God was moving in their lives. The Lord was stirring the calling He had placed in Christian's life. He would tell us so many things the Lord was showing Him. It was such a blessing seeing how God was using him.

Then Jon decided when he got out of the service, he wanted to moved back to Carlisle, Pennsylvania, and Sharon told us she was going to go with him. They left in May, and when summer came and the boys were out of school, we went to Pennsylvania too, to meet his family. They planned the wedding for the following year. While we were there, we fell in love with Pennsylvania. It was such a change from the desert, which we were more than ready to leave. We decided to move our home base to Carlisle, if it was the Lord's will.

We returned to El Paso and planned to put everything up for sale and give away what didn't sell. At the same time, we received a call from San Francisco to go and preach at a church we frequently visited. We traveled there with Ben and Josh. David stayed behind in El Paso; he was studying and working and didn't want to leave. Our family was growing up and going off on their own paths.

At home in the pulpit, preaching in Los Angeles

CHAPTER TWENTY SIX
"An event that changed our nation"

We had just finished a week of services in the San Francisco area. We were scheduled to leave on a flight back to El Paso. We woke up early, as we were suppose to be at the airport by eight that morning. It was September 11th. A friend called on the phone to tell us not to go to the airport, but to turn on the television. The news was saying that a plane had crashed into one of the Twin Towers in New York City. As we stood there watching the smoke coming from one of the towers, to our horror, a second plane flew into the other tower. All the world remembers the images of that day. We began to pray as news filtered out that these planes had been hijacked, along with another plane and then another. All flights were grounded. We watched as a plane crashed into the Pentagon, and then another went down in Pennsylvania. I didn't know how close to Sharon it had gone down. It seemed we were at war on our soil!

I remember calling David in El Paso and Sharon in Pennsylvania, to let them know we were not on the plane as planned. We were safe in San Francisco. Sharon told me the plane had not gone down near where she was living. Still, who knew what would happen next. All we wanted to do was to get home and have all our children safe with us. Sharon made me promise, if we could rent a car, that we would drive back to El Paso on back roads and not go through any major cities. No one knew what was coming next and if the attacks would continue in different areas.

Over the next few hours, we watched helplessly as the tower collapsed, and we collapsed in prayer before the screen, praying for all those people who were inside. It was as if the whole nation stopped.

I remember talking to my mother over the phone to let her know we were alright, and she said it was like Pearl Harbor all over again. No one knew what the next few days would hold.

We managed to find one car left at a car rental location and went to get it. We made the trip back with the radio on, listening for every update we could find. We prayed and cried the whole way back. God had spoken to me about our nation being tested, being shaken, and I wondered if this was what He meant. I remembered the vision I had years before when I was in New York. Now the vision had become reality. I saw as the firefighters were searching through the rubble, with their gas masks on, looking for survivors. This was no vision, it was reality. Yet in the midst of this horror, I saw a nation begin to turn to God. It was so sad to see that it would take something like this to bring them back to Him. There was so much loss and suffering, and yet, from it all courage and faith were born. Unity was born. What was meant for our destruction, was what God was using to make us strong. Churches began to fill, and even U.S. Senators stood on the Capitol steps and sang Amazing Grace. We would not be defeated! We would return to the God of our forefathers and seek His Grace. God was taking all things and turning them for our good, because we were called as a nation by Him, to carry the gospel to the ends of the earth. We hoped that a great revival would break out from this tragedy.

With the events happening in New York, many remembered the word God had given me before, and doors began to open in the New York area again. We packed up as much as we could and left for Carlisle. It was only three hours from New York, so it would be a good place to stay and travel back and forth from. We left the house to

David, and he had a room-mate. Our family was growing and moving on. Gone were the days when we all traveled in one car and were together continually. We were glad he would have Christian and Lily nearby, and after saying a tearful goodbye to them all, we hit the road towards Pennsylvania.

On the trip there, we stopped to visit our friends in Lafayette. We were invited to preach at Brother Ron's church, the Church of Acts. The ministry had grown there; they had a Bible college, and had started many "plant" churches. While we were there, Brother Ron told us he felt the Lord leading him to ordain us as ministers through his ministry. We were very humbled and blessed by this. We had ministered for years, taught seminars, held marriage conferences, developed discipleship courses, all as lay ministers. We knew God had called us, (that's what really counts), but we had never felt led to apply for ordination with any particular ministry or group. Being independent kept doors open to us to many different groups and denominations. We prayed about it, and felt confirmation. How fitting it was that my very first pastor would be the one to recognize our ministry officially and ordain us as ministers. He felt that our call from God, the years of experience, and our knowledge and ability to teach God's Word, met all the requirements for credentials as ministers.

He had a special ordination service for us. All our dear friends were there in support, and they came forward to lay hands on us and pray over us at the end of the ceremony. While they were all praying, brother Ron had a word from the Lord for us. He told us that the direction of our ministry was going to change. We would be established somewhere and would be called to pastor a group of people who would need us. We received this word with joy and felt it was confirmation of our move to Pennsylvania. We were now officially ordained ministers through Acts Global Outreach Ministries.

We arrived in Pennsylvania ready for God to open the new doors He had spoken to us about. We stayed with Sharon at first, and traveled back and forth to New York. The weeks turned to months. We rented a trailer home and began the preparations for her wedding.

It was a beautiful event by a river. It was a day we were thankful to be able to have. We were mindful of the two families who had lost their daughters and would never have the experience we were having. She was a vision. She looked like a princess with her flowing white dress and tiara on her head. She and her dad arrived in a horse drawn carriage, just like the princess stories she always loved as a little girl. We all fought back the tears as her dad walked her down the white satin walkway to a decorated arch at the rivers bank.

David was there, and Christian and Lily came. Stephanie and Katie were in the wedding as flower girls. It was a perfect day. Then a moment I will never forget, Sharon danced with her father. We came so close to losing our daughter, and now she was dancing with her daddy! It was a touching moment for us all. I think every one of us cried. Oh, God is so good!

Over the next months, the revival that was fanned by the events of September 11th, began to fade. People soon forgot and stopped going to church and seeking God as they had in those first months. So preaching engagements began to fade. Soon we were faced with no income, no work. Sergio decided to find a job. He had a degree in social sciences he could put to use. He found a job as therapeutic staff support for children with disabilities or behavioral issues.

I started to look for work as well. I applied serveral places, and then saw an ad for ABC-TV in traffic management. I always wondered why we had gone to El Paso, especially since it had come at such a high cost. Perhaps the training and experiences there were for some purpose like this. I applied at ABC in Harrisburg. I was the only applicant with previous traffic management experience. I went to the interview, and they all but assured me I had the job. They had some other interviews scheduled, but none of them had previous experience, so they showed me around, told me about the benefits, and said they would be contacting me at the beginning of the week. I was ecstatic!! What an opportunity, I thought. But then as I headed to the car after the interview, praising God all the way, the Lord put a check in my spirit. Suddenly, I felt uncomfortable about it and I began to pray. God told me I would not get the job.

I was disappointed, but prayed God would do His will as He always had done in my life. A couple of days later, I drove by a local restaurant, and to my surprise, God told me to go in and apply. I hadn't served tables since I was in High School, and now I was fifty years old! What would people think? I was an ordained minister, a person who had an international ministry, and now I was suppose to go work at a restaurant? Well, I decided the most important thing in my life was to please God, regardless of what it took or what others might think. After seeking confirmation, I went in and applied. The only job they had available was for a part-time server. Several days later, I got a letter from ABC thanking me for applying but they had hired someone else. The next day I got a call from the restaurant and they hired me. I had asked God to do His will, and so I put on a uniform and went for training.

We had visited a small church in Carlisle when we first came, but it was without a pastor, and not anything like the churches we were used to. When we returned the second time we started going to an Assembly of God church, but they didn't seem to need us for anything, and it was hard for us to just sit and not be serving. We remembered the small church for all the love they had showed and when we met the new pastor a year later, we decided to return to the church. He seemed delighted to have us there. He was very open to whatever we could do to work with him. Before long, I was nominated to be the leader of evangelism and outreach for the church. Sergio started visiting the local prison. I started a mid-week Bible study. I always believed wherever God plants you, you're suppose to bloom.

At work I had opportunities to meet people from all over the community. Before long the owners allowed me to start a devotional time before we opened. Doors opened to share my testimony with people on almost a daily basis. No, I wasn't in the pulpit, or in front of a camera. I wasn't famous or important. None of that mattered. I was content to serve the Lord. I realized how hard it was to spend a hard day at work, wearing yourself out, with family responsibilities, and pressures, and still find a way to serve the Kingdom of God. I was learning first hand how most people live. For sixteen years we had been in a "spiritual bubble". Now we were just like everyone else. It was a humbling experience. Did I have doubts? Did I think somehow I had been demoted, or failed in my mission for God, and therefore He had put me on a shelf somewhere? Yes, I battled all these fears and more, but through it all, I grew in spiritual maturity. I began to realize more and more that this life is not about what we do, it's about who Jesus is, and our becoming more and more like Him.

While working at the restaurant, Sharon had her first baby, a little girl that looked just like her. I was there at her birth. I thought of what a miracle it was to have her, and now another little girl like her. We found out later when she went for a check up that she was indeed a miracle baby. From all the x-rays and trauma from Sharon's accident, they said she would not be able to have children. But God is faithful, and He reserved a special little egg cell that wasn't radiated or affected, and gave us our little Paige Ellen.

We have finally settled, at least for now, if God doesn't tell us to move on again. Carlisle has been a wonderful place to raise our two youngest. They went to a great high school, away from the influences of gangs. They were actively involved in the church youth group all through their high school years. Ben became a leader at the Christian club through school and helped organize some of the "Meet you at the pole" prayer events. Joshua got involved in Young Life through school and went to their summer camp retreat. They both went on church youth trips to help build and repair houses for the poor.

Benjamin met a young lady, Mary Yeager, who became a Christian and eventually her whole family came to the Lord and became actively involved in church. They were married a year after graduation and are now expecting their first child.

Joshua graduated with honors and got a scholarship to Messiah College, where he is currently a sophomore with plans to study in England next year.

David moved from El Paso to Carlisle to be close to the family and found the love of his life, Gwendolyn Goforth. They are expecting their first child as well. He lives just two houses down from us. We are delighted to have the children still around us, well at least the four we had together. We have always been such a close knit family. After all, we spent years in a car, or sleeping in a hotel room together. Our children aren't just our children, they are our closest friends, and now we will be adding two more grandchildren to our family in 2011!

Christian and Lily moved to Albuquerque, New Mexico where he pastored for several years, and they are now actively involved in a large church that has many outreaches; he is helping them to develop a Spanish ministry. They adopted two young boys, Timmy and Kevin, and along with our granddaughters, Stephanie and Katie, together they are all busy for the Kingdom of God. I wish they were nearby as well, but I always knew God had something special for them to do, and they are doing it. They are such a close family, and great inspiration to many.

Sergi moved to Carlisle from Puerto Rico and is the father of two girls, Sophia and Heaven, and is studying to be an electrician. Liza remained in Puerto Rico, became a lawyer, a wife and mother of one girl, Eva Victoria. As for my son Chad, he is still absent from the family, but not from my heart. He is living in Tennessee at present with his wife. I still hold fast to the promise of God that the family will be united and serve the Lord together one day.

As for Sergio and I, we have been together over thirty years, and we are still deeply in love. Just as the Lord said so many years ago, we are far from perfect, but the love we have for each other has been a perfect love from the Lord that has helped us overcome all the obstacles we have faced in this life. Through it all, we have been the best of friends, always together, always there for each other. We have spent the last years here in Carlisle, serving God. We have developed outreaches to the local nursing homes, to the prison, as well as starting the first Spanish congregation in the city of Carlisle. I am the Associate Pastor at Lighthouse Church of God, and in 2010, published a book through Publish America, "The Kingdom Blueprint". It was a study the Lord led me to write about His eternal plan for His children and His creation. Then the Lord led me to write my first novel, which was published months later. It was a wonderful experience, something I had wanted to do ever since I started writing poetry when I was a young girl. Then the publishers contacted me about writing my story, and so I have put my life, my story, on the written page, in the hopes it will bring Glory to God, encourage the faith of many, and inspire others to "fall in love" with Jesus.

My life has been an amazing story of God's love and mercy, of His power and forgiveness. From the days of being a confused young girl who hated herself, God has taken me on this journey of service and self-discovery. He has changed me into a person who was useless into a servant who has served Him for over forty years. I love my life, and I love Him for giving me so many blessings and opportunities, but above all, I love Him for being the love of my life.

....And the journey continues!

I wish to thank so many people who have been a part of helping us. There are so many who housed us, worked with us, supported us, but most of all believed in us and befriended us. Of course, I want to first of all thank my wonderful family, whom God has blessed me with, but I also want to make mention of some special people who went out of their way to help us in our many travels back and forth.

Special thanks to:

- Dimas and Carmen Rodgriguez - Ministry coordinators in Puerto Rico
- Lalo Vergara — Ministry coordinator in El Paso/Juarez
- Oscar Sanchez — assistant coordinator in El Paso/New Mexico
- Cuahtemoch and Marisela Barcelo — Ministry coordinators in Los Angeles
- Hector Lugo — assistant coordinator in Los Angeles

Special thanks also to:

- Yiye Avila, for giving us an opportunity of a lifetime, for being faithful to God's leading, and forbelieving God sent me.

To those who housed us on numerous occasions:

- Eduardo and Maria Escobar
- Aquiles and Alejandra Jirau
- Herman and Coni Sanchez
- Jose La Torre
- Nick and Tita Morales
- Nicolas and Minina Naveira
- Cesar and Maritza Galindo
- The Aranda family
- Sandra Rodriguez
- Ivan and Eileen Diaz
- Bruce and Mary Freeman
- Paula Clifton
- Auder and Julia Aldana
- Reinaldo and Odalys Guerra
- Alfred and Nancy Figueroa
- Patricia Gonzalez
- Robert and Wanda Tirado
- Jofrey and Elia Vivoni
- David Vargas
- Awilda Burgos
- and the many others who helped us in so many ways.

Special thanks as well to all the many pastors and congregations who invited us to minister in their churches, and to all the people who supported our television and radio programs throughout the years.

Would you like to see your manuscript become a book?

If you are interested in becoming a PublishAmerica author, please submit your manuscript for possible publication to us at:

acquisitions@publishamerica.com

You may also mail in your manuscript to:

**PublishAmerica
PO Box 151
Frederick, MD 21705**

www.publishamerica.com